The Mystery of Transformation

Murray Stein

CHIRON PUBLICATIONS • ASHEVILLE, NORTH CAROLINA

www.ChironPublications.com

Cover image and design by Diane Stanley

Interior and cover design by Danijela Mijailovic
Printed primarily in the United States of America.

ISBN 978-1-68503-071-1

Library of Congress Cataloging-in-Publication Data

Names: Stein, Murray, 1943- author.
Title: The mystery of transformation / Murray Stein.
Description: Asheville, North Carolina : Chiron Publications, [2022] | Includes bibliographical references. | Summary: "The transformation of personality is mysterious, whether it comes about gradually or suddenly. In part, it is the result of the process of aging. Life itself puts a person through a series of transformations similar to the moultings of insects and reptiles. There are also rituals created by humans in their cultures that facilitate transformations to higher levels of identity and consciousness through instigating a process of spiritual death and rebirth into a greater sense of wholeness. The essence of the process is alchemical and what controls it is mysterious, lodged in the unconscious dynamics of the self. The chapters in this book are attempts at exploring those dynamics while acknowledging that they will forever remain beyond our understanding, a mystery. This work consists of a series of probes into the mystery of the individuation process. Central to the discussion are Jung's late writings on the alchemy of psychological transformation in the late stages of individuation"-- Provided by publisher.
Identifiers: LCCN 2022032372 (print) | LCCN 2022032373 (ebook) | ISBN 9781685030698 (hardcover) | ISBN 9781685030711 (limited edition paperback) | ISBN 9781685030681 (paperback) | ISBN 9781685030704 (ebook)
Subjects: LCSH: Individuation (Psychology) | Personality. | Jungian psychology.
Classification: LCC BF175.5.I53 S86 2022 (print) | LCC BF175.5.I53 (ebook) | DDC 150.19/54--dc23/eng/20220822
LC record available at https://lccn.loc.gov/2022032372
LC ebook record available at https://lccn.loc.gov/2022032373

Table of Contents

1. The Mystery of Transcendence — A Dream for Our Time   1

2. Dante's *Divine Comedy* — A Journey to the Mystery of Transformation   19

3. The Marriage of Anima and Animus in the Mystery of Individuation   55

4. "The Piano Lesson" — Wolfgang Pauli's Mysterious Union of the Opposites   101

5. *Mysterium Coniunctionis* — "The Mystery of Individuation"   121

6. Individuation and/vs. Enlightenment   161

7. The Mystery of Creativity — A Journey in Pictures   177

8. The Meanings of "Meaning"   197

9. The Faith of the Analyst   219

References   237

List of Paintings by Diane Stanley

Alchemical Sky © / Cover Art
The Inner Courtyard © / 6
The Eternal Fire Within © / 7
Beatrice © / 30
The Love that Moves the Sun © / 50
The Piano Lesson © / 120
Unio Naturalis © / 158
Unio Mentalis © / 158
Unio Mentalis et Soma © / 159
Unus Mundus © / 160

List of Illustrations

Ox-Herding Pictures, Public Domain / 171-176
Rosarium Philosophorum Pictures, Public Domain / 63-100

Acknowledgments

I wish to acknowledge the great debt of gratitude I owe to Diane Stanley not only for the brilliant artistic pieces she created for this book but also for her constant support and patience throughout the long process of writing and editing it from start to finish. Without her inspiration, this book could not have come into the light of day, and without her steady hand, it would likely have languished in the shadows of my busy life. I wish also to thank Steve Buser and Jennifer Fitzgerald of Chiron Publications for their dedication to publishing so many of my works and for their support specifically in bringing this one to fruition. They are an effective team and a most friendly one.

The Mystery of Transcendence — A Dream for Our Time

Introduction

Dreams sometimes give us a hint of mysteries ineffable. They present us with numinous symbols and are what Jung called, in his homely Swiss fashion, "big dreams." Such dreams offer us symbols that surpass our common understanding. Symbols are more than metaphors for something known or visible. They take us into a realm of the mysterious unknown and perhaps even the unknowable.

Such a dream was brought to me by a person who is, by her account, a seasoned spiritual practitioner. Among her many and varied practices over the course of 50 years, she combined many journeys to the East, lessons there from noted spiritual masters, intensive meditation, and Jungian psychoanalysis. All of this went into the construction of the spiritual and psychological dwelling place that she occupies today. This dream shows her the result of that work and takes her up to a level that opens suddenly and by surprise.

She has carefully written out the dream in as much detail as she can recall and offers as well associations to various features in the dream, some personal history as background for the dream, and some thoughts about the meaning of this dream for herself. She has also created some images to depict the structure of the house that is the container of the remarkable symbols in the dream. I will let her speak first and then comment on the dream.

. . . .

The Dream

I'm walking up the stairs in my house and am surprised that they continue on to a 5th floor which I have never seen and didn't know existed. I open the door, and there is a fire in the middle of a large empty room. The fire is surrounded by a low square grate. I'm concerned about smoke & a fire in the house, so inspect it more closely. There is no fuel—none at all. The fire is self-sustaining. How can this be? My mind stops. I'm in the presence of something mysterious. The light from the fire fills the room.

I notice the floor is rough, unsanded floor boards.

I go back to the entrance door. The "One Who Knows" or "Expert" appears at the door and looks into the room. We are both gazing at the fire together from the doorway. He says, "This is genuine. Put a carpet on the floor. Leave the door open. People will be coming to see this."

Dreamer's Associations and Initial Thoughts

The "expert" is someone who has appeared in several dreams, and often during critical transitions in my life. The central fire itself is breathtaking and stops me in my tracks. The room is empty yet full of otherworldly Presence. Nothing needs to be done to finish this fifth floor, except to install a carpet for the comfort of people who visit. "The One Who Knows" advises me to leave the door open for those who "will be coming to see this." I am willing to follow his advice but am still pondering its meaning.

Dreamer's Active Imagination: A Tour of the Dream House

In active imagination, I explored the first four levels of the dream house, upon which the fifth floor rests. The house is on the deep foundation of the cellar, but I enter on the first floor, walking into the kitchen and pantry. There is also a dining and living room with piano and comfortable chairs and sofa. It seems to be the *maternal level* of my house—comfortable and nourishing. In the accompanying drawing, I depict it as a series of evolving circular shapes.

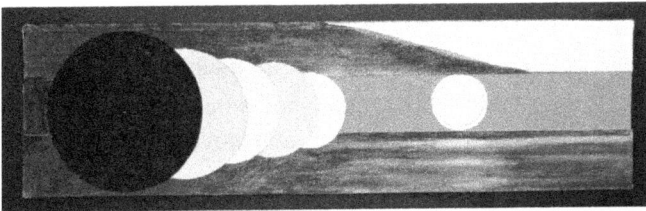

On the second floor is an office with computer, phone, file cabinet, bulletin board, notices, and to-do lists. This is the floor of work and responsibilities. It feels like a *paternal* sphere; the facts of collective life in the world. I have represented it as a black and a white square facing each other in a relationship that includes necessary tension.

On the third floor is the bedroom and library, an intimate place of ongoing transformative relationship. It is also an area of deep study, new ideas, sleep, and dreams. For me, this is my contemporary experience of the primordial energies of yin and yang.

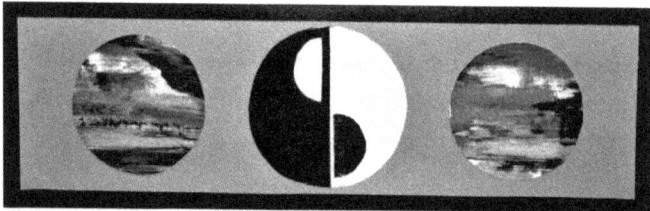

On the fourth floor is my art studio. It is filled with paints, brushes, canvases, paper, and a fine sound system for classical music. Above all, it is a creative space. Here, the dialogue of conscious and unconscious creates unexpected images and symbols. I drew this as all kinds of distinctive things held within a circle and a square. The square is bordered on each side by four lines, the bottom being black.

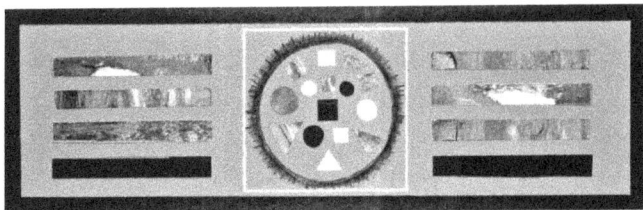

Finally, the *newly discovered* fifth floor has nothing to do with the personal aspects of the other four. It is self-illuminating, self-perpetuating, and self-revealing. It stands apart yet pervades everything.

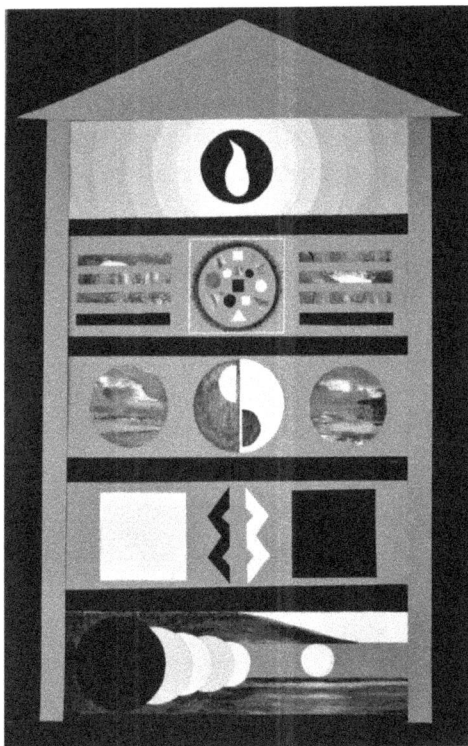

Five-Story House

Some Personal History as Context for the Dream

I have been a Buddhist practitioner for over four decades, studying closely with eminent masters. This obliged me to undertake regular daily practice and solitary retreats, as well as travel to India, Tibet, Nepal, and Bhutan on many occasions. I have also had a long-term and deep interest in Jungian depth psychology, including several years of analysis. My education and work experience is in the field of fine arts.

Further Reflections on the Fifth Floor

The fire is actually the center of the house, not "the top of the house." It is for me an ever-shining Source and the Heart of Being. The other living areas are arranged around it like a courtyard in a clockwise direction.

The Inner Courtyard

The Eternal Fire Within

When the eternal fire within is contemplated, it is found to be utterly mysterious, yet clearly present; transcendent, yet intimately connected to everything.

> "Illuminating inside and illuminating outside—a thousand illuminations; myriad illuminations; but in totality one illumination." (*I Ching*, Li, Fire)

....

My Comments on the Dream

I do not want to go into an extensive discussion of the nature and purpose of Jungian dream interpretation here, but a few words are necessary. The general procedure in this method of interpretation is to: a) establish the text of the dream; b) collect personal associations to persons and

7

images in the dream; c) consider the context of the dream (day residue, its place in a dream series, biographical data); d) amplify symbolic material in the dream; and e) bring the compensatory meaning of the dream back to the dreamer's immediate psychological state of mind. In this case, we have the dream text, some personal associations to the dream, something of the dreamer's context, and the dreamer's further work on the dream using active imagination, emotional responses, cultural associations, and artwork. What I would like to add and contribute are some further amplifications and my reflections on the dream as compensatory to contemporary culture.

In my view, this is a dream with a message for many, as indicated within the dream itself by the Teacher figure's words to the dreamer. The dreamer's willingness to share this dream with the general public by offering it for publication here is in line with the directions given by the Teacher to "leave the door open" for whoever can benefit from entering the room and from coming into meditative contact with the self-sustaining fire in the center, which is a "living symbol."[1]

When attempting to grasp the meaning of a true symbol, such as we find in the self-sustaining fire in this dream, it is worthwhile to consider a couple of sentences on the topic from Jung's last book, *Mysterium Coniunctionis*:

> If symbols mean anything at all, they
> are tendencies which pursue a definite
> but not yet recognizable goal and
> consequently can express themselves

---

[1] C.G. Jung, *Psychological Types*, CW 6, para. 819.

> only in analogies. In this uncertain
> situation one must be content to leave
> things as they are, and give up trying to
> know anything beyond the symbol.[2]

Jung is speaking about symbols as a feature in the process of unconscious thoughts becoming conscious. His is also a cautionary word about reducing a symbol to known meanings. It should remain a mystery, at least to a degree. Jung is working from an Aristotelian sense of entelechy, i.e., goal-directedness. The question to this dream would be: What is the aim of discovering an upper room with a self-sustaining fire in its center? Where is this dream tending? What is its goal? Jung says that we will have to be content in the end with simply living with the symbol as image because the unconscious thought it is tending toward is not yet available for conscious appropriation. The dream's final meaning cannot be specified at this time. But prior to resting in that contemplative attitude toward the dream symbol, one can amplify the image with analogous images from a wide spectrum of sources. After that, one can consider how this symbol might speak as compensation to the one-sided cultural attitude in which the dreamer and the dream are embedded. This will give some hint of the dream's intention.

To begin, I will consider the image of a self-sustaining fire. It is a symbol, which means it is the best possible representation at this time of a still unconscious content. The hermeneutic effort attempts to expand the self-disclosure, or revelation, somewhat further through amplification but not to explain it fully in rational terms.

---

[2] C.G. Jung, *Mysterium Coniunctionis*, *CW* 14, para. 667.

Jung notes the association of the alchemical Mercurius with fire: "He is *ignis elementaris, noster naturalis ignis certissimus*, which again indicates his 'philosophic' nature. The *aqua merculialis* is even divine fire. ... He is an 'invisible fire, working in secret.' ... He is, in fact ... 'the universal and scintillating fire of the light of nature, which carries the heavenly spirit within it.'"[3] As Jung interprets Mercurius, he represents the spirit of the unconscious, indeed a mystery.

The self-sustaining fire in the dream references the supernatural. This fire discloses a godlike presence in the dreamer's house and represents the inexhaustible energy of the Self. It is not "of this world," where all fires large and small eventually burn out and die away. Even the sun will eventually expire. This fire is rather of another order altogether. It is not dependent on anything but itself. It is mysteriously and infinitely self-sustaining. In theological religions, this is the definition of God. This is what distinguishes the Creator from finite creatures, who are radically dependent on many things for their sustenance. This fire is a symbol that offers an intimation of another dimension. The self-sustaining fire is a revelation, a "signal of transcendence" to use the phrase of Peter Berger.[4]

Another important feature in the dream is the *motif of discovery*. Dreams of discovering a new room or section of one's house are frequent and serve as indicators that an unconscious aspect of the personality is being made available to consciousness. Sometimes this indicates the breakthrough of

---

[3] C.G. Jung, "The Spirit Mercurius," *CW* 13, para. 256.
[4] See Peter Berger, *A Rumor of Angels: Modern Society and the Re-Discovery of the Supernatural*, Anchor, 1970.

a repression barrier or defensive wall in the psyche, but in this dream, it indicates rather the opening to a level of the psyche that had been previously unknown to exist. It is a revelation. From the dreamer's history and associations, it seems quite clear that she has been long preparing for this discovery. Still, it comes as a surprise to the dream ego, and the fire is at first seen as a possible danger to the rest of the house. The danger would be an outbreak of uncontrollable energy, an all-consuming mania that would burn the whole house down. But when she discovers that the fire does not consume anything at all and is self-sufficient, she is reassured and becomes curious. The house is safe. So what is this phenomenon?

A fire that flames upward but does not consume the underlying substance defies our normal and rational assumptions about nature. It is unnatural, and it draws our attention in wonder and amazement to itself. When Moses discovers a bush on Mount Horeb that is on fire but is not consumed, he is at first amazed and then becomes curious:

> And the Lord's messenger appeared to
> him in a flame of fire from the midst
> of the bush, and he saw, and look, the
> bush was burning with fire and the bush
> was not consumed. And Moses thought,
> "Let me, pray, turn aside that I may see
> this great sight, why the bush does not
> burn up."[5]

That this type of fire appears on the fifth floor of the dreamer's house suggests that the space is located in what the

---

[5] Exodus 3:2-3. Translation by Robert Alter.

philosopher John Hicks aptly names "the fifth dimension,"[6] a spiritual realm. It is "the Lord's messenger" who appears to Moses in the flames, namely an Angel. According to the biblical account, this fire is precisely where the Divine reveals and identifies Itself. The nonconsuming fire is a *numinosum*, a *mysterium tremendum et fascinans* in Rudolf Otto's words.[7] When Moses stops to marvel at the burning bush, the Lord calls out to him, and a conversation ensues between them. From the Voice out of the fire, Moses receives a commission, namely the command to "bring my people the Israelites out of Egypt."[8] At the climax of the encounter, there comes a revelation for the ages:

> And Moses said to God, "Look, when I come to the Israelites and say to them, 'The God of your fathers has sent me to you' and they say to me, 'What is His name?' what shall I say to them?" And God said to Moses, "'*Ehyeh-'Asher-'Ehyeh*, I-Will-Be-Who-I-Will Be.'"[9]

Thus is revealed the nature of Divinity in the form of a Holy Name and charged with absolute Will. As symbolized by the supernatural fire in the burning bush, moreover, God is shown as self-sustaining, atemporal and nonlocal — in short, beyond the time-and-space continuum.

In the dream under consideration, the dreamer does not receive this supreme a degree of divine revelation, but she

---

[6] J. Hicks, *The Fifth Dimension: An Exploration of the Spiritual Realm*, Oneworld Publications, 2013.
[7] R. Otto, *The Idea of the Holy*.
[8] Exodus 3:10.
[9] Exodus 3:13-14. In the more familiar King James translation of the Bible, this reads: "And God said unto Moses, 'I AM THAT I AM."

does get direct access to the realm of transcendence. And like Moses, she does also receive a mission: to offer entry to this mystery on the fifth floor of her house to others.

The number 5 represents the special quality of this space: It is the *quinta essentia*, the essence of the underlying quaternity. Jung writes: "... the four elements are converted into one another or synthesized in the quintessence. ... [The quintessence is] the most complete union of opposites that is possible."[10] More than a mere addition to the four lower levels, the fifth is a transcendent reality that brings the whole into a state of integration and unity. The four become One in the fifth. The dream suggests that the dreamer has gained entry into the mystery of wholeness. With the fifth floor, the house becomes a symbol of psychological wholeness.

What we as guests are invited to contemplate in this space of the fifth dimension is a psychological reality beyond temporality and limited location. This is something radically other than the time-and-space world in which ego-consciousness normally operates. The world that we know with our senses and through scientific observation is limited by the ego's awareness of causality and entropy. A fire must be fed by fuel in order to continue to burn, and when the fuel is consumed, as it must be, it will die. This is a fixed law of nature. Even the stars will eventually consume themselves in their fires and go dead.

I once climbed a steep hill with a friend on the sacred island of Miyajima in Japan up to a Shinto temple on the summit that contained a fire that had been kept burning continuously for 1,000 years, according to the local records

---

[10] Jung, *Mysterium Coniunctionis*, *CW* 14, paras. 310-11.

and the attending priest's testimony. It was deeply moving to stand before this small fire in a sacred space and contemplate its longevity. With incredible devotion, the priests had kept this fire going through all the tumultuous history that had swirled around it in that time — national wars, natural disasters, even the atomic bomb that had been dropped on nearby Hiroshima in 1945 — and to this day they humbly fed the fire regularly and ritually, to keep it alight. But this fire, long-lived as it is, has to be fed by fuel external to itself. It is not self-sustaining. Because it has been kept going for such a long time, it suggests the numinosity of an eternal flame, but actually, it belongs to the world of time and space. There is an external cause for its continuing existence. It has to be fed. In the Fifth Dimension, the fire is neither caused nor fed by a source outside of itself. This is a mystery, beyond scientific understanding.

There are many symbols of the eternal in the myths of the world, but a self-sustaining fire suggests a specific type of energy, namely Eros. In typological terms, it is an expression of the feeling function: heat, passion, and transformational energy. Among the organs within the subtle body, it is the heart that would be associated with fire. The Eternal Fire is the type of Divine Love that Dante experienced in his ultimate vision of the Godhead at the end of his journey through the realms of the afterlife. Suddenly, he was struck as if by lightning, he writes in *Paradiso*, and he absorbed into his own being "the Love that moves the Sun and the other stars."[11] The poet is utterly transformed by this exposure to Love Divine. The eternal, self-sustaining fire in the Fifth Dimension represents

---

[11] Dante, *Paradiso* XXXIII:146. Translation by John Ciardi.

precisely this and nothing less: Divine Love. This is what people are being welcomed to experience in the house of the dreamer. Even though it is an impersonal room — it has no furniture, no pictures on the walls, no knickknacks — it intimates intimacy because it exists in her house, not in a public space.

The door to the fifth floor opens the Fifth Dimension for the dreamer as well as for guests who visit the room. This is the realm of the timeless unconscious above, not beneath, the floors of the temporal psyche. It is the realm of Mercurius, the great transformative agent of alchemy, of whom Jung writes that this is "an 'invisible fire' working in secret,"[12] whose activities affect the entire house on all levels. Important to realize, however, is that all five floors are features of one house, the dreamer's. The fifth story is an aspect of the dreamer's wholeness even though it goes beyond the personal. There is only one house, but it has layers and dimensions.

One assumes that the fifth floor has always been there and is only now being discovered. For the dreamer, a door is opened to a realm of psyche that has been present and active all along but until now perceived as elsewhere through the extraordinary phenomenon of projection, into faraway exotic places and teachers. The dream brings consciousness into the location of the numinous eternal flame as an inner reality. "As above, so below": God is above and within. This is what Jung calls the fifth stage of consciousness.[13] The projected Deities of the religious traditions have disappeared from the external

---

[12] Jung, "The Spirit Mercurius," *CW* 13, para. 256.
[13] *Ibid.*, para. 248.

world and are now found within the psyche as archetypal images and powers.

The house is one. Jung's attempt to construct a unified worldview that includes the time-space continuum with the principle of causality along with "indestructible energy" and "synchronicity" in a single reality (one house) was worked out with the Nobel Prize-winning physicist and mathematician Wolfgang Pauli.[14] The house of this dream is a representation of that equation. The basement and first four floors represent temporality, the dreamer's life in time, which extends from the subbasement of the primordial world of animal instinct up through the cultural and personal unconscious levels and through the psychological developments represented (as described) in floors 1-4. Above this temporal structure is the fifth story, which houses the Eternal Fire — the infinite, the supernatural, "indestructible energy." It is all one house, not two. Temporality and eternity are joined in a single unified whole in the life of the individual. This is an image for our times. This is a dream for our times.

In Switzerland, where I live, houses are often named for something that was historically associated with the place. The office I use in Zurich is in a building named zum Schwanen — "of the Swans." Down the street and across the river, there is a lovely hotel named, Hotel zum Storchen ("Hotel of the Storks"). This dreamer's house may be named, with her permission, "The House of the Eternal Flame" ("*das Haus zur ewigen Flamme*"). Those who enter this house and are invited up to the room at the top will have an opportunity to see the self-sustaining fire. This energy is not sourced in

---

[14] See Jung, "Synchronicity: An Acausal Connecting Principle," *CW* 8, para. 963.

the material world of gas and oil. It is sourced in a realm beyond temporality. In effect, the archetypal is in residence in the individual personality. This is where we now experience the eternal and the nonemporal: The individual personality has become a *temenos*, a sacred space. The archetypal and the individual are one substance.

After living with the dream of eternal fire for a considerable period of time, the dreamer had another dream following up on this one, which indicates a further step in her individuation process and is an important message for others who might also catch a glimpse of the existence and location of the Fifth Dimension.

> *I dreamed of entering a Christian church, a Vedic temple, and a Buddhist monastery. All three were familiar and inviting, but then in the dream, I remembered the central fire and thought, "I don't need to be here in any of these religions anymore. The living fire is within."*

For the dreamer, the discovery of the room on the fifth floor of her house represents an initiation and a completion of becoming conscious of what is within. But this insight does not complete her work. She receives a command from the figure named Teacher: "Leave the door open for others to enter." It seems that her house has become a temple and her inner world a treasure to be shown and shared. This is the basis for the invisible spiritual community that today is becoming global.

Dante's *Divine Comedy*: A Journey to the Mystery of Transformation

Prelude

Dante's *Divine Comedy* has been my constant companion for some time now. I'm finishing this essay in February 2021 at my home in Goldiwil, Switzerland, where I have been sequestered during the coronavirus pandemic that has cast its shadow over much of the world for the past year. In this dark time, I've read Dante's poem in several English translations and with ever-increasing wonder at the depth of psychological insight contained in it. Now more than ever I understand the immense dedication of the many distinguished scholars who have spent their entire professional lives studying this work. Once hooked by the magnificence of *The Divine Comedy,* one is never free of its power to charm and teach. Dante uniquely captures and recasts the entire known world of his time in his poem. It is a novel creation much like the biblical Lord's of the world in six days. Dante has here transformed the whole extent of classical and Christian cultures into a personal artifact with an inimitable signature. As a whole, it is beyond my comprehension, so deep and complex and all-embracing is its differentiated coverage of this world and the next.

A point of meaningful coincidence at this specific time in history is that the problems Dante confronted in his world are so similar to ours. The hostile political and social divisions that afflicted Florence in his time are equally present in our contemporary world, where an unrestrained lust for power has extinguished the possibility of cooperative community life. We are as split in our politics as Florence was in the days of Guelfs and the Ghibellines 700 years ago. Where there is only power, love is absent: That was Dante's problem, and it is ours. Dante found his way to a brilliant solution for himself by taking an inner path through an imaginal world. I believe that if we carefully read his narrative, we will discover suggestive ways for tackling our own dilemmas. We might even find a cause for hope. A deep reading may even instigate a psychologically transformative experience in the reader.

The Divine Comedy is a magnificent artistic expression of psychological and spiritual transformation as experienced within the specific context of Dante's medieval culture. His poem represents distinct stages of an individuation process in the form of a journey through three imaginal spaces called Inferno (Hell), Purgatorio (Purgatory), and Paradiso (Heaven). It is this psychological development in the narrative that I am interested in highlighting here. I am not a Dante scholar and have read this magnificent work of art only in translation. I am therefore sadly deaf to the musicality of its poetic language, even though some of it can be heard distantly in the excellent translations that are available in English. Moreover, I am acutely aware that the depth and precision of insight that this work offers are beyond my powers of description. In this sense, I feel much like Dante did when he confesses that his imaginal experiences are often beyond his ability to capture in words. The poem takes us into feelings and shows us images that are indefinable and beyond our powers of description in language. It induces a kind of cognitive arrest.

It is for all these reasons that I must venture cautiously into an exploration of these deep waters, but I proceed with the hope that I may catch some of the poem's most essential psychological developments in the net of the Jungian theory of individuation. Can *The Divine Comedy* teach us something significant and relevant today about the individuation process in the second half of life? And can the theory of individuation help us to understand *The Divine Comedy* more profoundly? I trust the answer to both questions will be affirmative. I would like to think of my endeavor here as a dialectical exchange between a literary work and psychological theory, each contributing something important to the discussion of individuation and each learning from the other.

Introduction

In his late work, *Mysterium Coniunctionis,* C.G. Jung describes three stages of psychological development that occur typically in the second half of life. It begins with a crisis at midlife, which shatters the previously honed persona with its finely attuned cultural attitudes and its dedicated orientation toward specific goals of social and professional achievement. Often this crisis is initiated by a dramatic loss — of a social or professional position, of a loved one, of an idealized person, or a cherished belief system — after which a period of disorientation and disillusionment sets in. Jung experienced this crisis at the age of 37 following the break in relations with Sigmund Freud, and Dante experienced it at about the same age following his exile from his home in the city of Florence. Whereas Jung's individuation journey did not conclude until his death many years later at the age of 86,

Dante's ended with his death at the age of 56 in Ravenna and shortly after completing *The Divine Comedy*.

What we find in Dante's masterpiece is a singular account of a strange journey through the lands of the dead that presents a remarkable story of individuation in the second half of life. It is a pilgrimage that clearly reveals increasing degrees of psychological and spiritual development as the protagonist advances. The main character in the story, i.e., the figure of the pilgrim Dante, experiences a journey of individuation, while at the same time Dante as poet transforms this process into a work of art. Like Jung crafting his *Red Book* over more than a decade, Dante composed *The Divine Comedy* over a similarly long period of time, from 1308 until 1321 as scholars have estimated. Although he claims that the experience he is writing about took place in only a few days while he was in Rome during Holy Week in 1300, he spent the next 20 years thinking and writing about it in order finally to create the poem as we have received it. Both Dante's exceptional psychological gift for visionary experience and his remarkable literary talent for poetic expression go into making the work of art that we know as *The Divine Comedy*.

The story is told as a recollection of an experience in the past that Dante is only later recounting in the poem. It is not impossible that the core experience he is writing about took place in a short space of time. The account of it, however, took much longer to compose. It is a brilliantly burnished jewel of a poem that displays the strictest control of form — exactly 100 Cantos equally divided into three Canticles (*Inferno, Purgatorio, Paradiso*), the first with an extra Canto that serves as the introduction, and all of it written in "the

preternaturally strong Italian terza rima,"[1] a poetic form that
Dante invented specifically for this work. The story contains
a complex mixture of events and personalities from Dante's
life and times, plus many classical Greek and Roman figures,
plus biblical and religious characters, as well as images and
stories offered often with shock value and surprise by his
imagination. The result is one of the greatest works in all
of world literature; the psychological result of the journey
is what I will speak of as transformation in the course of
individuation.

As a Jungian psychoanalyst, I am looking at *The
Divine Comedy* not primarily as a work of art but as a record
of psychological transformation achieved through what
we today call active imagination. The poem is a record of
an individuation process that begins at midlife in a state of
confusion and darkness (a *nigredo* state, in the language
of alchemy), then moves through a long series of imaginal
confrontations with shadow figures and themes and advances
by rigorous reflection and analysis to reach an *albedo* state
(in alchemy known as "the whitening"). Finally, it arrives
at *rubedo*, the brilliant "reddening" in the alchemical opus,
which signals that alchemical "gold" has emerged from the
transformed *prima materia* that was placed in the vessel
at the beginning of the process. This transformation in the
alchemical vessel mirrors the simultaneous psychological
transformation of the alchemist, in the poem of the poet.
Dante is not only writing *about* a process that he is observing;
he is all the while participating *in* the process he is writing
about.

---

[1] I borrow the phrase from Harold Bloom in *The Western Canon*, p. 82.

These stages of alchemical transformation correspond to the phases of individuation described by Jung in the final chapter of *Mysterium Coniunctionis*, "The Conjunction," where he explicates the psychological meaning of the alchemical process as described by the alchemist Gerhard Dorn. Dorn describes three stages of alchemical union, or *coniunctio,* as: 1) the separation of soul from body (a state of *unio naturalis*) and the subsequent union of soul and spirit (a state called "*unio mentalis*") with the body left behind and out of the picture (this is the *nigredo* phase); 2) the (re)union of *unio mentalis* with body, which marks a transformation of body (the *albedo* phase); and 3) the union of this synthesis of body, soul and spirit with *unus mundus*, a transcendent reality (the *rubedo* phase). I will argue that the pilgrim Dante as portrayed in *The Divine Comedy* achieves the state of *unio mentalis* in the second Canticle, *Purgatorio* (stage 1). He proceeds from there with Beatrice, who leads him through the fires and waters out of Purgatory and into Heaven, where his body becomes a subtle body, which represents a union of *unio mentalis* and body in a new synthesis (stage 2). In his new body, Dante is not subject to gravity, and he casts no shadow. In Heaven, he receives spiritual instruction from various illustrious teachers and undergoes a series of strict examinations that qualify him for the final numinous visions of the Celestial Rose and the Holy Trinity. It is beyond these that an electrifying moment of transformation occurs, which creates a permanent union with *unus mundus* (stage 3). The net result of his imaginal journey is individuation in the highest degree. This is the psychological lens through which I am reading *The Divine Comedy.*

Did the man, Dante Alighieri, really have the profound transformative experiences that he describes so convincingly in his work? If so, did he have them before he wrote about them, or did he have them while he was composing the poem? As the poet tells the story, he is looking back in faltering memory to experiences that took place in Rome during and shortly after Holy Week in 1300. *The Divine Comedy* could well be based on a series of intense visionary experiences that Dante had during that brief period of time, which supplied him with the *prima materia* for the later carefully structured and intellectually worked-out literary masterpiece. To the original experience, he would have added material that amplified it and gave it further body and detail. In the completed work, then, Dante would be giving an account of a core visionary episode that occurred in a short span of time, like a week, which took years of reflection and imaginative elaboration to render in the full amplitude of breadth and meaning that it implied. The final product is clearly the result of a long process of cognitive digestion, which may well be based on an overwhelming numinous experience that occurred during those spiritually charged days of Easter weekend during the Jubilee Year that had been called for by Pope Boniface VIII for 1300.

The multitude of details in the poem is far too numerous to consider here. The selection of scenes and characters that I have chosen to focus on are what I see as some of the critical turning points of significance in the individuation journey depicted in the poem. I do not intend this to be primarily a psycho-biographical study of Dante's personal psychological and spiritual development, but rather to consider the poem as a deeply considered expression of a process that has archetypal sources of energy and whose movement is driven and directed ultimately by the Self. Without question, Dante's psychological development and his work as a poet were deeply intertwined, as was the case with alchemists and the transformational processes that they were attending in the laboratory. *The Divine Comedy* is a testament to psychological transformation as an archetypal process, but doubtless it is the story of Dante Alighieri's personal transformation as well.

Act 1: The Journey through Hell — *Nigredo*

In the alchemical understanding of human nature as expressed by Gerhard Dorn, there are three basic aspects: body, soul, and spirit. Initially, the soul has a strong inclination to fuse with the body, and at the conception of a human being, it does so and thereafter clings to it compulsively. This is called *unio naturalis*. This union is ordained by nature. The term "body," however, also has a broader meaning in that it includes the entire phenomenal world. The soul's attachment extends beyond the physical body to the mother in the first place and later to all of material and physical existence. This includes the person's entire social, economic, professional, and political life. The "body" to which the soul is attached becomes the whole horizontal dimension of life in the world. The soul becomes totally absorbed in all of this, and for a time knows of nothing else.

This is Dante's condition before his crisis at midlife and his subsequent imaginal journey through the three regions of the afterlife. His consciousness was totally immersed in his life as a physical man, as a prominent member of an important family in Florence, as a political figure in his community, and

26

as a courtly love poet of increasingly great renown. He was intensely attached and committed to his immediate world, and his energy was engaged to full capacity in a multitude of meaningful daily activities. Body and soul, in the alchemical sense, were wed in a tight embrace. This does not mean that he did not experience some minor traumas and setbacks in love and work, but on the whole, his life showed a successful progression on the levels appropriate to the first half of life.

What remains left out of this close union of body and soul, according to Dorn, is the third element, "spirit." Spirit is Logos in the high sense of the word. It connotes Truth and ultimate Meaning as opposed to social or temporal meaning. Attachment of soul to body brings a sense of meaning on the mundane and horizontal plane through being active in worldly affairs, but it does not offer meaning on the spiritual plane. The world of spirit hovers above the soul/body couple and is alien to it.

The Self in the Jungian sense of the word demands greater consciousness than is offered on the horizontal plane. Psychological identification with one's time, place, practical tasks, persona, and so forth is the natural result of development in the first half of life, and this is succeeded by further stages of individuation in the second half of life. It is this further development that the alchemist Gerhard Dorn refers to as the creation of *unio mentalis*, which is a union of soul and spirit, now with body left behind. This stage of development requires, first of all, the separation of soul from body, pictured as death in alchemical imagery. This brings about the *nigredo* phase of the process, the beginning of the second half of life individuation. The movement toward *unio mentalis* is initiated when the soul's habits of investment in life

27

are frustrated and thwarted by events on the horizontal plane — failures, illness, death of loved ones. The individuation journey begins with a rupture in the established patterns of life, which results in a plunge into a mental state of confusion and radical psychological alienation from what has been a familiar world of persona identity and activity.

The Divine Comedy opens dramatically precisely at this moment of crisis. The poet wakes up in a dark wood, lost, and finds his way blocked by dangerous animals. He cannot get past them in order to return to his home and the familiar surroundings where his identity has been forged and located. In the opening lines of *The Divine Comedy*, Dante retrospectively recalls this terrifying moment:

> Midway in our life's journey, I went
> astray from the straight road and woke
> to find myself alone in a dark wood.
>
> How shall I say what wood that was! I
> never saw so drear, so rank, so arduous
> a wilderness! Its very memory gives
>
> a shape to fear. Death could scarce be
> more bitter than that place![2]

Jung would speak, albeit somewhat reluctantly, of this critical moment in life to his young students at the Swiss Federal Institute of Technology (ETH) in Zurich, as one familiar with its psychological challenges:

> I really should not stress this turning
> point in front of so many young people,
> it does not concern them and yet perhaps

---

[2] Dante, *The Divine Comedy: Inferno* 1:1-6.

it is as well that they should know it. A
point exists at about the thirty-fifth year
when things begin to change; it is the
first moment of the shadow side of life,
of the going down to death. It is clear
that Dante found this point. ... When
this turning point comes people meet it
in several ways: some turn away from
it, others plunge into it, and something
important happens to yet others from
the outside. If we do not see a thing Fate
does it to us.[3]

Dante plunged into it, as did Jung when he went through the
experiences depicted in his *Liber Novus*.

Fortunately for Dante, a guide appears as he grows ever
more desperate: the poet Virgil emerges from the shadows.
He has been sent as an emissary by Dante's archetypal anima,
his soul, the beloved Beatrice, who has observed his fearful
condition from afar in her place in the transcendent realm of
Heaven. She begs Virgil to go to Dante's assistance in the
sweet tones of a beloved:

> "O gracious Mantuan whose melodies
> live in earth's memory and shall live on
> till the last motion ceases in the skies,
>
> my dearest friend, and fortune's foe,
> has strayed
> onto a friendless shore and stands beset
> by such distresses that he turns afraid

---

[3] C.G. Jung, *Modern Psychology*, p. 223.

from the True Way, and news of him in
Heaven
rumors my dread he is already lost.
I come, afraid that I am too-late risen.

Fly to him and with your high counsel,
pity,
and with whatever need before his good
and soul's salvation, help him, and
solace me.

It is I, Beatrice, who send you to him.
I come from the blessed height for
which I yearn.
Love called me here.[4]

Beatrice

---

[4] Dante, *Inferno* 2:58-72.

The intervention by Beatrice and the guidance of Virgil will prove decisive in Dante's journey. Without their help, Dante would have been consumed spiritually in a hopeless standoff with powerful instinctual forces that block his progress: three threatening beasts that block his way to the summit. One is a lion, a symbol of pride, presumably Dante's own and also that of his opponents in Florence; the second is a leopard, a symbol of lust and hopeless attachment to the pleasures of the flesh, to which Dante was especially prone; and the worst of all is an insatiably hungry she-wolf sent from Hell by Envy, a symbol of avarice. The she-wolf is never satiated, and in fact, she becomes hungrier the more she eats.

Dante is helpless and knows of no way to get past these primitive forces in his nature, which would keep his soul locked in place and hopelessly entangled in futile conflicts within himself and with others interminably. He is baffled about how to proceed in life, but Virgil makes a suggestion: "He must go by another way who would escape/ this wilderness."[5] This other road will lead to a descent into the darkest shadows of the underworld and from there ascend to realms of transcendence beyond the limits of rational knowledge. This is what we would today call an individuation journey of psychological transformation through the realms of the unconscious to the Self.

Virgil will guide him onto a path that will take them into and through the underworld. This descent follows the classical pattern of the hero's journey as described in

---

[5] *Ibid.*, 1: 89-90.

Homer's *Odyssey* and Virgil's *Aeneid*. It is also the path into the unconscious that Jung writes of in *Liber Novus*.

At the outset, Virgil gives Dante a preparatory description of the journey ahead. First, he tells him, they will pass through the shadow world of Hell, where he will "see the ancient spirits tried/in endless pain, and hear their lamentation/as each bemoans the second death of souls."[6] The people in Hell are there forever, and their torment is eternal. They wait without hope for the "second death," which will take place on the Day of Judgment. From Hell, the poets will make their way to Purgatory, where he will "see upon a burning mountain/souls in fire and yet content in fire,/ knowing that whensoever it may be/they yet will mount to the blessed choir."[7] This journey through the realms of shadow where souls are forever locked in place (Hell) and where other souls who are undergoing purification (Purgatory) will bring them to the entrance of Heaven, where "a worthier spirit shall be sent to guide you,"[8] says Virgil, namely Beatrice, the transcendent anima.

In the journey through Hell, Dante discovers what happens when individuation is rejected as an option in life. The scenes show the consequences of compulsive and unrepentant (unreflected) attachment of soul to body. These are people who in life refuse to let go of the objects of their wanton passions or even attempt to free themselves from the force of their desires. They represent the psyche that resists the development from *unio naturalis* to *unio mentalis*. Dante

---

[6] *Ibid.*, I: 108-110.
[7] *Ibid.*, I: 111-114.
[8] *Ibid.*, I: 116.

frequently feels sympathy for them. Who wouldn't? Isn't it natural to refuse the invitation to greater consciousness? This is the lamentable human condition, as everyone knows. Dante is also horrified at what he sees. Were it not for Beatrice and Virgil, he might well be stuck here, too, forever blocked by pride and lust and devoured by the she-wolf of avarice.

It must be acknowledged that the separation of soul from body is emotionally wrenching, an *opus contra naturam*, as Jung writes about it when he describes the challenges facing the person who attempts it:

> Since the soul animates the body ... she tends to favour the body and everything bodily, sensuous, and emotional. She lies caught in "the chains" of Physis, and she desires "beyond physical necessity." ... the separation means withdrawing the soul and her projections from the bodily sphere and from all environmental conditions relating to the body ... the disciple will have every opportunity to discover the dark side of his personality, his inferior wishes and motives, childish fantasies and resentments ... in short, all those traits he habitually hides from himself. He will be confronted with his shadow ... He will learn to know his soul, that is, his anima and Shakti who conjures up a delusory world for him.[9]

---

[9] C.G. Jung, *Mysterium Coniunctionis*, para. 673.

Separation of the soul from the body precedes a later union and is the precondition of further individuation. This is a tall order, and as humans, we are naturally lazy and prefer to retain our habits of feeling and acting.

Among the most poignant scenes that Dante encounters as he travels through this dark world occurs in the Second Circle of Hell, where he comes upon the adulterous lovers, Francesca and Paolo. Francesca is a sympathetic image of the soul's passionate attachment to the object of her desire. She reminds Dante of his own sensuality and love of life in the body. In sharp contrast to Beatrice, who also died young and was taken directly to the highest realm of Heaven, Francesca is consigned forever to the dark chambers of Hell because she refused to separate from her lover, the brother of her husband. Even in Hell, she retains the image of a beautiful young woman, and she shows no remorse for her adulterous love for Paolo, laying the blame for the affair on romantic poets. Love seized Paulo first, she says, and she responded powerfully: "Love, which permits no loved one not to love,/took me so strongly with delight in him/that we are one in Hell, as we were above."[10] Sensual love is a folly hard for Dante to condemn. In much of his previous poetry, he, too, had sung the praises of courtly love, which celebrated precisely this type of amour. Francesca tells him in graphic detail the touching story of how it happened that she and Paulo became lovers while reading a poetic account of Lancelot's guilty love for Guinevere, and then she cries out: "That book, and he who wrote it, was a pander."[11] Meanwhile, Dante

---

[10] Dante, *Inferno* V: 100-103.
[11] *Ibid.*, V: 134.

hears Paulo quietly weeping nearby and is overcome with emotion: "I felt my senses reel/and faint away with anguish. I was swept/by such a swoon as death is, and I fell,/as a corpse might fall, to the dead floor of Hell."[12] Dante is overcome both by guilt for himself being such a pander and by feverish identification with the passion of the lovers.

After this, it is hard for Dante to move on, yet he does so, albeit with obvious anguish. His steady guide, Virgil, who is traditionally taken to represent reason, presses him to continue the journey. The transformation from *unio naturalis* to *unio mentalis* is assisted by, in Jung's words, "… the help of the spirit, by which are meant all the higher mental faculties such as reason, insight, and moral discrimination."[13] This is Virgil. And, beyond that, Virgil will lead Dante to figures who represent "… a 'window into eternity' and … convey to the soul a certain 'divine influx' and the knowledge of higher things,"[14] as we shall see in the figures of Beatrice and St. Bernard in the third Canticle, *Paradiso*.

I am reluctant to draw a parallel to psychoanalytic work, but the temptation is great to observe that Virgil functions much like an analyst who accompanies a client through retrospective shadow realizations. In studying *The Divine Comedy,* I have been fascinated by the figure of Virgil. As an analyst, I feel a sense of kinship with the part he plays in serving Dante as a witness, a guide, and a voice of encouragement when the anguish of guilt and shame mount like the furies Dante feels all about him as he passes through the awesome gate into Hell:

---

[12] *Ibid.,* V: 137-140.
[13] C.G. Jung, *op. cit.,* para. 673.
[14] *Ibid.*

> Here sighs and cries and wails coiled
> and recoiled on the starless air, spilling
> my soul to tears. A confusion of tongues
> and monstrous accents toiled
>
> in pain and anger. Voices hoarse and shrill
> and sounds of blows, all intermingled,
> raised tumult and pandemonium that still
>
> whirls on the air forever dirty with it as
> if a whirlwind sucked at sand.[15]

This resembles moments in analysis when the prospect of encountering shadow material in its full reality is more than a little frightening, and the reassurance of the analyst, who knows this territory, has a soothing effect that allows the journey to go on. Similarly, Virgil explains the source of the voices crying out and urges Dante to continue on the way through Hell and then into and through Purgatory. It is a long and necessary journey through all the shades of shadow realization that precedes the eventual crossing over into the next stage of transformation.

Why is this necessary? Why can't Virgil just find an easy way to bypass all this misery, to take Dante straight up to Heaven, and once there, to turn him over to Beatrice for a pleasant flight into his beatitude? The truth is that there are no shortcuts to individuation. In the now many years of working as a Jungian psychoanalyst, I have occasionally seen the unhappy consequences of this attempted leap over the shadow into what was claimed to be "liberation" or

---

[15] Dante, *op. cit.*, III: 22-29.

"enlightenment" or "true self" and "higher consciousness."
It is an aged person's sad story. The denial and avoidance
of shadow do not eliminate it. Looking away from the
problems presented by a threatening confrontation with the
shadow looks like an easy solution in the short distance, but
the person will later arrive right back at the starting point
of the journey. In fact, time may run out, and people will
remain stuck in the shadowland of hopeless suffering and
despair, like the souls Dante observes in the circles of Hell.
The separation of soul and body must be faced and worked
through — deeply, painfully, patiently — in order to prepare
the soul for its union with spirit in *unio mentalis*. That is the
work shown to the poet and his guide in *Purgatorio*.

Act 2: The Journey through Purgatory — *Albedo*

In the alchemist Dorn's depiction of the achievement
of *unio mentalis*, there is first an imperative to separate soul
from body, which is followed by the union of soul and spirit.
The first is a moral achievement; the second is a commitment.
In Dante's *Divine Comedy*, the first step takes place by
observing carefully the shadow figures in Hell and registering
their suffering and the reasons for their placement there.
They show the consequences of keeping the soul attached
to the body to the very end of life. This leg of the journey
is followed by the passage through Purgatory, where Dante
witnesses and himself experiences the process of separation
of soul from body, step by step.

The exit from the shadow realm of Hell requires
facing ultimately what Jung named "absolute evil."[16] This

---

[16] C.W. Jung, *Aion*, para. 19.

confrontation is depicted in the descent to its frozen bottom where a three-headed Satan, the shadow of the Holy Trinity whom Dante will encounter in Heaven, is sealed solidly in ice. It means looking absolute evil in the face, which is, as Jung writes in his late work, *Aion*, "a shattering experience" ("*erschütterende Erfahrung*").[17] When Virgil shows Dante the figure of Satan and tells him, "Now see the face of Diss! This is the place/where you must arm your soul against all dread," Dante stammers: "Do not ask, Reader, how my blood ran cold/and my voice choked up with fear. I cannot write it."[18] Some commentators have speculated that Dante nearly went mad at this stage. Virgil, the steady guide and emissary of the divine Beatrice, takes Dante close to himself and slips down the frigid body of the "Emperor of the Universe of Pain" whose "upper chest [jutted] above the ice."[19] When they reach the level of Satan's thighs, their direction suddenly reverses, and the way down becomes the way upward. This rather dizzying turn at first disorients Dante, for now suddenly, they are ascending and making their way upward through a narrow passage where they find themselves at the top of the world. Hell is now forever beneath them, and the rest of the journey is an ascent into the light. We now enter the stage of the alchemical *albedo*.

Until now Dante has been a mostly passive witness of the shadow figures who are locked in place forever in Hell. He engages in conversations with the damned, but he is not required to take a more active part in the journey. Entry into

---

[17] *Ibid.*
[18] Dante, *Inferno* XXXIV 20-23.
[19] *Ibid.*, XXXIV: 31.

Purgatory, however, calls for his participation, for active commitment with consequence. At the entrance to Purgatory, they meet Cato, the archetype of the moral hero from Roman times, who instructs them on how to proceed. After that, they come upon three large, colored steps at the gate to Purgatory, which call for heartfelt contrition (white), confession (black), and ardor for good works (red).

Unlike Hell, which is static, Purgatory is dedicated to change. As in Hell, there is suffering, but here there is the promise of advancing from level to level, culminating in access to Heaven. The shadow traits that must be confronted in Purgatory are represented by figures who are being slowly and meticulously transformed. Whereas the passage through Hell showed Dante the consequences of soul clinging compulsively to body, the journey through Purgatory becomes a master class in shadow confrontation and separation of soul from body. And Dante actively participates in this class.

In the antechamber to Purgatory, they find the lesser sinners: The Excommunicate, The Lethargic, The Unabsolved, and Negligent Rulers. In Purgatory proper, they find seven levels of more serious but still hopeful sinners: The Proud, The Envious, The Wrathful, The Slothful, The Avaricious, The Gluttonous, and The Lascivious. Each type of moral turpitude must be transformed through the purgatorial process and replaced by the corresponding virtues: humility, mercy, peace, solicitude, generosity, abstinence, and chastity. Each of these successive processes calls for an additional degree of separation of soul from body and a deeper union of soul with spirit, thus moving the individual along toward *unio mentalis*. In diagnostic terms, this involves transformation of shadow aspects and features of character disorders such as pathological narcissism and borderline tendencies. This is a statement of an ideal outcome. As anyone who has been in long-term analysis knows, this process of encountering the shadow is an ongoing work and takes immense stamina and commitment. The ego's self-protective defenses resist violently. Purgatory is a place of salutary and meaningful suffering, unlike the suffering that we see in *Inferno*.

As the angel of God who stands on the red stair at the top of the staircase makes ready to allow the poet's entry to Purgatory, Dante is surprised: "Seven *P*'s, the seven scars of sin/his sword point cut into my brow. He said:/ 'Scrub off these wounds when you have passed within.'"[20] These marks will be expunged as he ascends through the levels of Purgatory, and their removal will serve as certification that he has achieved the corresponding virtues. This will be evidence that he has achieved a high level of *unio mentalis*. Dante is now fully engaged in the process of transformation.

Accompanied by Virgil, Dante climbs successively through all seven levels of Purgatory. Along the way, he speaks at each circle with one or more of the souls located there who are being slowly and painfully purged of their sins. For them, it takes incredibly long periods of time — years or centuries. For Dante, it moves much more quickly. As the wounds on his forehead are washed away one by one, he can advance. The treatment is swift and effective in Dante's case. He seems to get the message at each level and thus finds himself released from the attachment that would hold him there.

Finally, Heaven is practically in sight, and the two pilgrims hear the angels singing in the near distance. But

---

[20] Dante, *Purgatorio*, IX: 112-114.

before Dante can pass over into that ultimate destination, he
must undergo the test by fire. An angel announces: "'Blessed
ones, till by flame purified/no soul may pass this point.
Enter the fire/and heed the singing from the other side.'"[21]
Dante shivers with dread and is understandably reluctant
to go forward as he vividly remembers a scene he had
once witnessed of burned bodies. But Virgil reassures him
("'Within that flame/there may be torment, but there is no
death'"[22]), so hesitantly he finally steps into the flames:

> Once in the flame, I gladly would have
> cast my body into boiling glass to cool it
> against the measureless fury of the blast
>
> My gentle father, ever kind and wise,
> strengthened me in my dread with talk
> of Beatrice, saying: "I seem already to
> see her eyes."[23]

The ordeal in the refiner's fire is the final stage in the forging of
unio mentalis as a stable state of consciousness. It is a critical
moment in the process of transformation. The alchemists
would have called this operation *calcinatio*, the treatment by
fire that burns away the metal's dross and impurities.

Following this point, Virgil will take his leave:

> "Expect no more of me in word or deed:
> here your will is upright, free, and whole,
> and you would be in error not to heed

---

[21] *Ibid.,* XXVII 10-12.
[22] *Ibid.,* XXVII: 20-21.
[23] *Ibid.,* XXVII 49-54.

whatever your own impulse prompts
you to: Lord of yourself I crown and
mitre you." [24]

Virgil's leave-taking from the pilgrim Dante is for me one
of the most touching scenes in *The Divine Comedy*. It is a
moving blessing given by the archetypal father poet to the
younger. Dante has now arrived at a stage of development
that frees him from the need for Virgil's further guidance. He
is now free and on his own. No longer confused as he was
when Virgil first approached him in the dark wood; he can
now fully trust himself and his impulses. The union of soul
and spirit has been accomplished, and Dante is now prepared
to take the step into the final leg of his journey to fulfillment.

Act 3: The Journey through Heaven — *Rubedo*

When Dante leaves the realm of unresolved shadow
as depicted in the *Inferno*, he enters Purgatory, where light
again prevails as it does at dawn. Whereas Hell represents
the psychological state of resistance to becoming conscious,
Purgatory is equivalent to *albedo* in the alchemical process,
a realm of increasing movement toward consciousness and
transformation. As Dante is about to leave Purgatory, he
is met by the transcendent anima figure of Beatrice. The
anima's role is to link ego-consciousness to the Self. She
has performed this role so far through her emissary, Virgil,
and now she will take Dante into Heaven. This is the *rubedo*
stage in the alchemical transformation process — where base
materials (*prima materia*) transform into alchemical gold

---

[24] *Ibid.*, XXVII 139-143.

Who is Beatrice? Dante's Beatrice was a young girl in Florence whom he fell in love with when he was 9 years old, and after that, he saw her only occasionally and mourned her death when she passed away in her 20s. From the first moment, she was a symbol of his anima. How and why she was taken up to Heaven straightaway upon her death and installed among the highest saints in the Mystic Rose in close proximity to the Virgin Mary herself is unexplained and a mystery. This elevation is a unique creation of Dante's imagination. Harold Bloom writes of Dante's bold creation in his inimitable fashion: "Nothing else in Western literature ... is as sublimely outrageous as Dante's exaltation of Beatrice, sublimated from being an image of desire to angelic status ..."[25] Sublimation (*sublimatio*) is a familiar process in alchemy, referring to the transformation of base materials (*prima materia*) to the *lapis philosophorum*, alchemical "gold." This is what has happened to the human figure of Beatrice. She has become an exalted symbolic representation of the anima archetype. On the base level, the anima is a spinner of illusions through the psychological mechanism of projection, but at another stage of development, she is the go-between of ego and the self. This is the anima as we see her in the figure of Beatrice in *Paradiso*. For Bloom, a literary critic, this transformation is "sublimely outrageous," but for a Jungian psychoanalyst, it is not so strange. Beatrice, once human, has in death become archetypal, and now in the inner world of the psyche, she takes the form of a subtle body and inhabits the realm of symbolic reality. As anima in this sense, Beatrice now becomes Dante's guide and will take him over

---

[25] H. Bloom, *The Western Canon*, p. 72.

the threshold to the center of the Self, which is represented in *The Divine Comedy* as the Godhead.

In order to join Beatrice in her transcendent world, the pilgrim Dante must himself undergo a process of sublimation and also become a subtle body. This occurs toward the end of *Purgatorio* when he is immersed in the river Lethe, which purges him of his past, and then drinks deeply of the waters of the river Eunoë, which restores him to his original primal essence. Here, Dante achieves full *unio mentalis*: His body, which until now has cast a shadow, changes into a subtle body that is transparent and is no longer subject to gravity. His soul is now united with the spirit, and this unity is represented in a new transfigured body. When soul commits absolutely to spirit, consciousness is transformed. It participates in life as a subtle body and participates in a "fifth dimension," as it is sometimes called by contemporary philosophers of religion.[26] The celestial figures Dante encounters in *Paradiso* are quite different from the physically vivid figures portrayed in *Inferno* and *Purgatorio*. They are visible but more ephemeral. Jung quotes the alchemist Dorn concerning this transformation of the body:

> At length the body is compelled to resign itself to, and obey, the union of the two that are united [soul and spirit]. That is the wondrous transformation of the Philosophers, of body into spirit, and of the latter into body, of which there has been left to us by the sages the saying, Make the fixed volatile and the volatile fixed, and in this you have

---

[26] J. Hick, *The Fifth Dimension: An Exploration of the Spiritual Realm.*

> our Magistery. Understand this after the
> following manner: Make the unyielding
> body tractable, so that by the excellence
> of the spirit coming together with the
> soul it becomes a most stable body
> ready to endure all trials. For gold is
> tried in the fire.[27]

Dante still has some trials ahead of him.

Although Beatrice is a symbol of Eros in the highest
sense of the meaning of Love, she speaks surprisingly in the
exalted language of Logos as she instructs Dante and shows
him the sublime architecture of the universe. At this stage of the
journey, the poet Dante goes beyond memory and poetic mastery
(as expressed by the presence of Virgil) and employs visionary
imagination that reveals the primal forms and structures of
Being, in short, the foundations of the collective psyche. This
is the world of archetype, entry into which is assisted, as Jung
writes, by "… the spirit [which] is also a 'window into eternity'
and … conveys to the soul a certain 'divine influx' and the
knowledge of higher things …"[28] This visionary state of mind
is mediated by Beatrice. Dante's imagination here is of the type
that Henry Corbin describes in the writings of Sufi mystic, Ibn
'Arabi. Corbin argues that this type of imagination reveals,
objectively, the invisible spiritual world:

> This manifestation [of God] is neither
> perceptible nor verifiable by the sensory
> faculties; discursive reason rejects it.
> It is perceptible only by the Active
> Imagination … at times when it

---

[27] Quoted by C.G. Jung, *Mysterium Coniunctionis*, para. 685.
[28] *Ibid.*, para. 673.

> dominates man's sense perceptions, in
> dreams or better still in the waking state.
> ... The "place" of this encounter is not
> outside the Creator-Creature totality, but
> is the area within it which corresponds
> specifically to the Active Imagination, in
> the manner of a bridge joining the two
> banks of a river. The crossing itself is
> essentially ... a method of understanding
> which transmutes sensory data and
> rational concepts into symbols by
> making them effect this crossing.[29]

In *Paradiso*, Dante engages this type of Active Imagination,
which goes beyond metaphor, transgresses the limits of
conscious mental capacities, and "shows" (*darstellen* = to
represent, to display, to reveal) an ultimate mystery. Jung
writes in this mode about the numinous visions he experienced
while recovering from illness in his later years:

> I would never have imagined that any
> such experience was possible. It was not
> a product of imagination. The visions
> and experiences were utterly real; there
> was nothing subjective about them; they
> all had a quality of absolute objectivity
> ... The objectivity which I experienced
> in ... the visions is part of a completed
> individuation. It signifies detachment
> from valuations and from what we call
> emotional ties.[30]

---

[29] H. Corbin, *Alone with the Alone*, pp. 188-89.
[30] C.G. Jung, *Memories, Dreams, Reflections*, pp. 295-96.

What Dante describes in *Paradiso* is a revelation of the subtle structure of the cosmos and its fundamental energic organization. Beatrice's lectures are geometric and have a degree of mathematical clarity and exactness. They resemble a university course in astronomy or physics, but they are delivered with a profound feeling of soulfulness, of love. In this, she symbolizes the sublime reality of *unio mentalis*, the union of soul and spirit, Eros and Logos, within the feminine form of a subtle body. Dante speaks of becoming "trans-human" (*"Transumanar"*[31]) in this realm. In a sense, he and Beatrice are bodiless, but more precisely they occupy an imaginal or subtle body, for they still have distinct form. They are figures of Active Imagination in Henry Corbin's sense of the term.

The Cantos of *Paradiso* that lead up to the final supreme revelation describe in careful order the various realms of all creation. There is an ascent from a space named Earthly Paradise through the circles of planets and stars and on to the exalted Empyrean. Once there, Beatrice shows Dante the wondrous Mystic Rose, crowned by the Virgin Mary and in which Beatrice holds a prominent rank. Suddenly, Beatrice vanishes, and Dante has a new guide, the famous medieval mystic and devotee of the Virgin Mary, St. Bernard. It remains now only to experience the ultimate vision of the Godhead. Dante's educational lessons in *Paradiso*, as delivered by Beatrice, the Apostles, and St. Bernard are all aimed at preparing him for this *ne plus ultra*, which is described in the 100th and final Canto of *The Divine Comedy*. This is the scene in which the third stage of the *mysterium*

---

[31] Dante, *Paradiso*. I: 70.

coniunctionis as outlined by Gerard Dorn and expounded by Jung is accomplished: the union of the body transformed by *unio mentalis* with the *unus mundus*. In Jung's view, "this would consist, psychologically speaking, in a synthesis of the conscious with the unconscious."[32]

Initially, St. Bernard signals to Dante that he should follow "the aura/of the high lamp which in Itself is true."[33] As the poet turns there and gazes steadily into that light, he has a glimpse of total Unity (the Self, in Jung's terminology):

> I saw within Its depth how It conceives
> all things in a single volume bound
> by Love, of which the universe is the
> scattered leaves;
>
> substance, accident, and their relation
> so fused that all I say could do no more
> than yield a glimpse of that bright
> revelation.
>
> I think I saw the universal form that
> binds these things, for as I speak these
> words I feel my joy swell and my spirits
> warm.[34]

It is a vision of totality that takes in at once all of history and its energic essence of love. As Dante gazes steadily into the light, some details emerge:

> Within the depthless deep and clear
> existence of that abyss of light three

---

[32] C.G. Jung, *Mysterium Coniunctionis*, para. 770.
[33] Dante, *Paradiso*, XXXIII 53-54.
[34] *Ibid.*, XXXIII 85-93.

> circles shone — three in color, one in
> circumference:
>
> the second from the first, rainbow from
> rainbow; the third, an exhalation of pure
> fire equally breathed forth by the other
> two.[35]

This vision of three circling spheres then further differentiates, and Dante sees a human form vaguely represented in one of them. As he gazes into this mystery, he hits the limit of his capacities and confesses: "...but mine were not the wings for such a flight," and then suddenly "the truth I wished for came/cleaving my mind in a great flash of light."[36] This sudden flash of visionary insight marks the final and supreme point of Dante's spiritual and psychological transformation — union with the *unus mundus*. The result is expressed in simple words because it exceeds the sublime language that even a master poet can inscribe in verse:

> Here my powers rest from their high
> fantasy, but already I could feel my
> being turned — instinct and intellect
> balanced equally
>
> as in a wheel whose motion nothing jars
> — by the Love that moves the Sun and
> the other stars.[37]

---

[35] *Ibid.*, XXXIII 115-120.
[36] *Ibid.*, XXXIII 139-141.
[37] *Ibid.*, XXXIII 142-146.

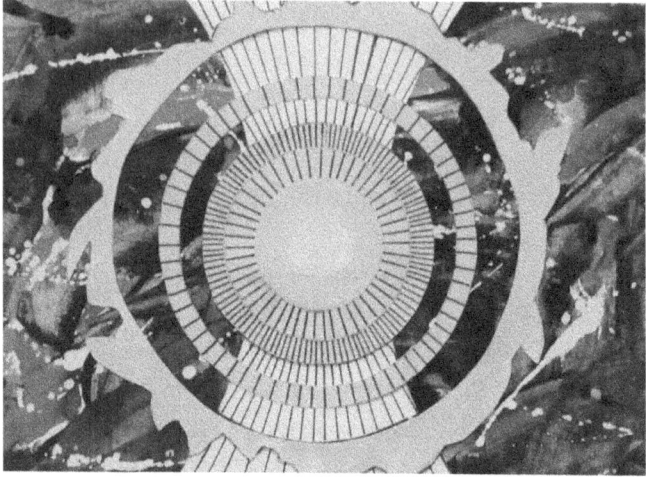

The Love that Moves the Sun

The poet cannot describe what he saw in this vision. It is beyond his imagination and verbal capacities. My impression is that he gazed into the very bottom of the collective unconscious, into the Self, where All is made One. But even more importantly, he experiences union with the Self and becomes invested with Love, its fundamental energy. Individuation has here reached its ultimate goal and is now complete to the extent that this is humanly possible.

Dante died on "the night of September 13 (1321), having just finished the final cantos of the Paradiso."[38] "Legend tells us that Dante was pointed out in the streets as the man who had somehow returned from a voyage to Hell, as though he were a kind of shaman."[39] One may add that

---

[38] T.G. Bergin, *Dante*, p. 44.
[39] H. Bloom, *The Western Canon*, p. 83.

in his poetic account of the journey through Hell, Purgatory and Heaven, Dante shows the readers of his poem just how far the process of individuation can extend. It begins in loss, confusion and fear; then passes through penitence, reflection and transformation; and finally attains the highest reaches of spiritual and psychological integration. This would make of Dante a true prophet and in the style of a master poet.

Postlude

The outcome of the three-stage process of transformation as described by Dorn and interpreted by Jung is a transformed personality, as *The Divine Comedy* so movingly depicts. As psychotherapists, we might wonder, given our experience in working with clients who are in the process of individuation, to what extent is this a real possibility? Or is this a fantasy — granted, on a high level, but fiction nevertheless? Does numinous experience in Active Imagination such as we find described in *The Divine Comedy* make a real difference in how people ultimately feel about life and themselves, in how they behave toward others, in how they formulate the meaning of life in the final analysis? Does the effect last, or is it only a momentary highpoint?

We do not know much about how the imaginal journey through the underworld and the afterlife (i.e., the unconscious) changed Dante Alighieri, the man. Did he become what he claims for the pilgrim in the poem? From my experience with Jungian psychoanalysts, I can testify that deep engagement with dreams and active imagination over a period of time does make a lasting impact on the lives of our clients. We also know that this process in analysis does not entirely remove the effects of early traumas and the consequent

51

complexes, although it does assist a person in outgrowing them and relativizing their effects on consciousness. The creation of an ego-self axis on the inner level shifts the locus of control from persona concerns about prestige and power to a type of selfhood that brings with it a considerable degree of loving acceptance of self and others. And beyond that, there are inner experiences that give one a perspective on life that frames personal experience in a more objective concept. In some cases, this makes the difference between choosing life over death. This would testify to the veracity of Dante's claim that one's being can be brought into harmony with the "Love that moves the sun and the other stars."

I prefer to understand the journey as described in *The Divine Comedy* in its totality — *Inferno, Purgatorio* and *Paradiso* — as a mandala that describes human wholeness. There are parts of the personality that are forever frozen in place and will never change (the figures depicted in *The Inferno*). These are intransigent complexes that continue to exist even in advanced stages of individuation. There are other parts that can be transformed like the figures in *Purgatorio*. These are amenable to change and are capable of undergoing transformation. And there are numinous parts of the Self in the archetypal realm of the psyche that are glimpsed from time to time in dreams and visionary experiences. These are the figures depicted in the exalted realm of Heaven in *Paradiso*. Ego consciousness can locate itself principally in any of these realms and may travel through all of them many times in the course of a long individuation process. It is possible that in later life, if a state of wisdom is achieved as described in Dante's poem, the predominant position will be fixed more or less steadily by the achievement of a union with *unus mundus,* and love and generosity will predominate in the conscious attitude.

In a conversation with the Zen Master Shin'ichi Hisamatsu, Jung, who was then in his mid-80s, was asked a sharp question after they had spent a good deal of time comparing the goal of Zen Buddhism, i.e., liberation from all suffering, with the goal of analysis, i.e., psychological wholeness. They had agreed that freeing a person from the suffering caused by the complexes, personal and cultural, and even from archetypal influences, was a common goal. The conversation then comes to a climax with this exchange:

> **SH**: From what you have said about the collective unconscious, might I infer that one can be liberated from it?
>
> **CGJ**: Yes! [40]

This produced a gasp of surprise among the people present. It was an astonishing response, given Jung's usually more modest estimations of human potential for individuation. What makes this important for our present reflection is that it suggests Jung's agreement that transformation of the type Dante describes in *The Divine Comedy* is psychologically possible, even if only for a moment. One can step out of personal history with its accumulation of complexes and cultural conditioning (by bathing in the river Lethe), attain to a transformed sense of self (by drinking the waters of Eunoë), and even go beyond the most sublime archetypal images imaginable (Beatrice, the Mystic Rose, the Holy Trinity) and be struck suddenly by lightning (the satori experience in Zen Buddhism, the ultimate numinous experience in *The Divine*

---

[40] S. Muramoto (tran.), "The Jung-Hisamatsu Conversation." p. 46.

Comedy), which transforms consciousness to such a profound degree that only the transcendent Self (God) and its Energy (Love) rule over it. This is a tall order, but no doubt other mystical traditions such as Cabbala, Sufism, and Kundalini Yoga would concur.

Even if not often seen in the outcomes of the individuation processes unleashed and fostered by Jungian psychoanalysis, the vision offered in Dante's poem can serve as an inspirational image for the goal of individuation.

The Marriage of Animus and Anima in the Mystery of Individuation

Individuation involves two main movements, separation and integration. Only that which has been separated can be united, states an alchemical maxim. In psychological development, it is the same: before union, distinction. This holds true for the classic pair of opposites, animus and anima. Their separation takes place in the first half of life, their union in the second. This article will focus on the latter while assuming the former.

The marital union of animus and anima is graphically depicted in the alchemical series of 20 woodcut images and accompanying texts titled *Rosarium philosophorum*. C.G. Jung used the first 10 images of the series to discuss the relational aspect of analysis in his work "The Psychology of the Transference." While he emphasized the process of integration as a relational matter, I will be focusing here primarily on the intrapsychic union and transformation of anima and animus within the psyche of each individual in the dyad. This integration of the opposites is a development that occurs simultaneously on both interpersonal and intrapsychic levels. The two aspects belong together and cannot occur alone without reference to the other. In this essay, I will go back and forth between the two aspects but give more emphasis and attention to the intrapsychic.

Commonly, this development is a stage of individuation that occurs in the second half of life. It is a process that dissolves the established one-sidedness of consciousness and produces a further level of psychological maturity through integration of a feature of the unconscious that we refer to as anima and animus. In turn, this development leads to contact and identification with the ultimate source of psychic life, the self. The *Rosarium philosophorum* tells this complex and fascinating story in pictures and accompanying texts.

A Theoretical Review

To begin, some discussion of terms and the unfolding stages of psychological development will serve as an introduction. The terms "anima" and "animus" refer to archetypal patterns of psychic energy that inhere at the level of the collective unconscious. Jung identifies them occasionally as the energies of Eros and Logos, i.e., connection-making and meaning-making energies. In using these terms, we are speaking about features of the psyche that are only minimally controlled by ego-consciousness but are energetically largely autonomous in their various manifestations. We can experience their influence in our spontaneous feelings and thoughts, also imagistically as figures in dreams and active imagination. They frequently affect our conscious attitudes — anima as intractable moods, animus as rigidly held opinions. Often, they manifest in projections onto others. We can find them graphically represented in imaginative literature, fairy tales, myth, film, music, opera, drama and so forth, where we are invited freely to project them onto culturally constructed figures and narratives.

In his writings, Jung often uses shorthand definitions: the anima as the feminine side of a man's psyche, the animus as the masculine side of a woman's psyche. But this rests on the cultural attitudes prevalent in his European culture when Jung was writing. I am going to consider them in a more strictly archetypal way, as both belonging to both biological genders. Anima and animus energies are common equally to both females and males. Their distribution and manifestations are psychologically determined, not biologically restricted or controlled. The diagram below illustrates the psychic setup.

O

OUTER WORLD

PERSONA

EGO

— —

PERSONAL UNCONSCIOUS

SHADOW

— — — — — — — — — — — — — — — —

COLLECTIVE UNCONSCIOUS

ANIMA   ANIMUS

This diagram applies to individuation without reference to gender.

. . . .

The account of the relationship between anima and animus begins with what Jung called "the syzygy" in his late work, *Aion*. *Syzygy* is Greek for "union" or "conjunction"; the term refers to an intimately linked pair, a twosome. They are two, but they exist as a single unit, like Siamese twins. In origin, anima and animus are two aspects of a single psychic constellation, having on one side the face of the animus and on the other the face of the anima. Similarly, Plato's *Symposium* tells a myth about the origin of human beings as being originally two-sided creatures. At some point, they are divided and lose contact with one another. Thereafter, they spend their lives looking for each other, longing to reunite and re-create the unity they once were. When they find one another, they reunite. We can think of the anima and animus with this model in mind when we consider them as part of the individuation process. Once they were together, then they were separated, and finally they come together again. This is a three-stage developmental process.

The basic idea is that when we are born, we come from the womb with a self that is complex but undifferentiated and at first mostly in a state of potentiality. This original self has been compared to an acorn, which contains all the germ material (potential) that will be used in the course of an oak tree's development. If you cut an acorn in half, you don't find a little tree inside that will grow big in time. You find the germ material that is the potential for growth into a full-fledged oak tree. It is the same with the original self: It comes into being when a mother's egg is fertilized by a father's sperm and a fetus grows into a human infant in a mother's womb. An individual is born with the psychological potential that will then become elaborated and develop into a full-fledged personality in the course of life. Taking his cue from alchemy, Jung speaks of this rich potential as *prima materia*, out of which the individuation process will eventually generate a human personality.

Jung conceives of the self as a mandala (a circle) with a center. The *prima materia* within the mandala is first of all in a "pleromatic state," i.e., there are no clear distinctions among the potential contents. It is a *massa confusa*, a kind of undifferentiated mixture of genetic elements. An energy, a "principal," then comes into play that Jung calls the *principium individuationis*. In the first of the *Septem Sermones ad Mortuos,* this principle is called "Creatura." It functions to begin differentiating the contents in the mixture and arranging them into pairs of opposites. Psychologically, the appearance of this function within the self signals the emergence of consciousness within the personality. Consciousness functions to make distinctions among objects and between oneself and others, inner and outer, good and bad, etc. It also divides the steady flow of time into past, present and future. Featured at the center of consciousness is the ego, the "I."

The animus and anima take form as a pair of opposites within the psychic matrix. This is the so-called syzygy.[1] At the beginning, the distinction between them is minimal, unnoticeable, even though they are two. In time, contrasts and differences develop, but the syzygy unit remains intact within the pleromatic state of consciousness that is present in infancy. As consciousness increases, the ego takes note of

---

[1] See C.G. Jung, "The Syzygy: Anima and Animus," *Aion*, *CW* 9ii.

differences and makes a selection of one of the pair to identify with more strongly. This separates animus and anima, and a degree of tension is created between them as they now divide and form two distinct energy patterns. What was one now becomes two. At first, there is some confusion and a mixture of attributes, but eventually, the anima and animus will emerge as features in the personality's energy distributions in their own particular ways: the animus as a type of active, separating energy, and the anima as a type of receptive, uniting energy. The one divides and makes distinctions; the other unites and harmonizes.

The energic quality of the animus is solar in its clarity and intensity, and as Logos, it defines and refines perceptions and thoughts as it seeks distinctions, form, and understanding. The energy of the anima, on the other hand, is lunar in its dimly lit intuition, and as Eros, it relates emotionally to people and objects and seeks to connect with them. The one tends upward to spirituality and mind, the other tends inward and outward to materiality and body. The animus is associated with the so-called masculine principle, the anima with the so-called feminine principle. In alchemy, they are represented as Sulphur and Salt. We should keep these differences distinct from biological gender differences. They are psychological and not biological components of ourselves. Everyone has both types of consciousness in the psychic repertoire. The difference is only that one becomes more prominent than the other in the character of an individual at a given time in the individuation process.

As an individual personality develops in the first half of life, the dominant attitude and identity that inform ego-consciousness show features more of the one than the other side of this polarity. After midlife, this changes, and both become more equally represented. It is important to keep in mind that these are archetypal energies and not personal dispositions only. That is, they transcend ego-consciousness and belong to the general level of human endowment. They are psychic principles that affect all human beings everywhere and throughout history. They influence us; we do not control them.

In the traditional enactments of human culture, young girls identify with the anima side of the syzygy and become representatives of it. They take this pattern of being human into their conscious self-image and feelings about themselves, first as little girls, then as young women, and later as mothers, matrons, grandmothers, and wise old women. They have a developmental trajectory based on their identity with the anima side of the syzygy. On the other hand, young boys traditionally take up the animus side of the syzygy and develop their identities and features of personality around it. When animus-identified-man meets anima-identified-woman and they develop an intimate relationship based on the projection of anima and animus, they are restoring in an outward fashion the unity of the original syzygy. We speak of them as "soul mates." The two separated halves find each other and come together again. This is a story of the reunion of anima and animus on the interpersonal level. It symbolizes a deeper story that takes place in the unconscious of each of them where his anima and her animus unite. Thus, the couple is actually a four-some, a conscious pair and an unconscious pair.

It should be added that this need not be the traditional man-and-woman pairing. In recent times and with LGBTQ gaining acceptance in many societies, the combinations can be quite different and rather fluid. They might be animus-identified-man and anima-identified-man, or animus-identified-woman and anima-identified-woman, or animus-identified-woman and anima-identified-man. Transgender couples add even more permutations. The restoration of the syzygy on the interpersonal level need not be reflective of gender differences.

This reunion on the interpersonal level is not all there is to this process, as I will speak of it in the next section of this article. If we consider the intrapsychic level, the interpersonal union is the beginning of a new chapter in the story of the process of transformation, which changes both individuals at the inner level. This is the story we can consider in the 20 pictures of the alchemical treatise, *Rosarium philosophorum*. We must keep in mind that inner reflects outer, and outer affects inner. They need each other. In other words, what we do in our interpersonal lives has a direct bearing on what happens in our inner lives, and vice versa. That's why Jung stated that a person cannot individuate by sitting alone in a cave or on a mountaintop. Human interaction is a necessary ingredient in this alchemical process.

An Alchemical Account of Marital Union Between a King and a Queen

The *Rosarium philosophorum* is an alchemical text that dates from the 16th century (ca. 1550 C.E.). It was composed and first published in Frankfort, Germany. There are a total of 20 pictures (woodcuts) in the work, which can be divided into four parts: 1-3, 4-10, 11-17, and 18-20.[2]

---

[2] Images from https://www.alchemywebsite.com/virtual_museum/rosarium_philosophorum_room.html

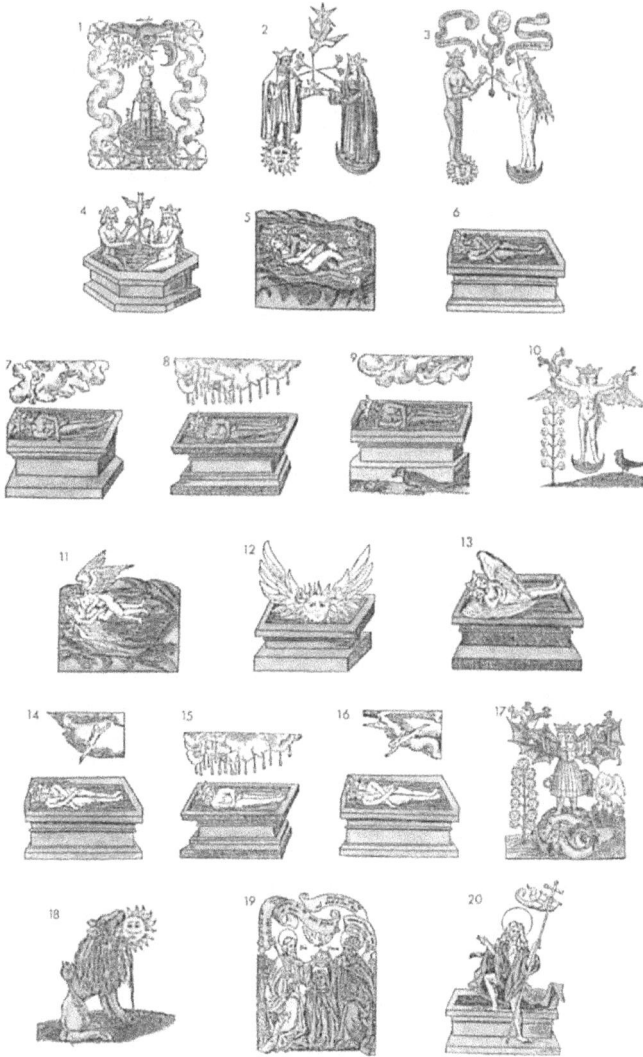

The first three pictures represent the preparation for the processes to follow. The next seven pictures (4-10) show the transformation of Queen Luna (the anima) with King Sol (the animus) accompanying her in this process. The next set of seven pictures (11-17) shows King Sol's transformation, with Queen Luna accompanying him. And the last three pictures (18-20), which represent the fourth and final movement of the process, depict transformation through death (18), elevation (19), and divinization (20). I will comment on the psychology of each stage of this process in detail as I consider the pictures one by one.

Picture 1: "The Mercurial Fountain"

"The Mercurial Fountain" is the place where the process occurs. The picture as a whole represents the transcendent self as container.

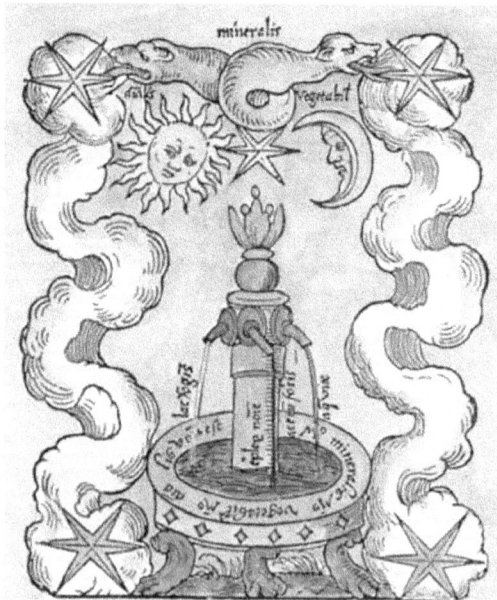

Whereas the stars in the four corners indicate the container's transcendent nature and dimensions, the alchemical process takes place also within a carefully constructed and bounded space — the alchemist's laboratory — for which the Adept must take responsibility. The Adept is both witness to and participant in the process. The space in which this takes place is a temenos, a protected area set apart from profane life. It is open to the depths of the unconscious but not to the surrounding social world. It is a private, inner space, and the procedure is akin to active imagination. In Jungian practice, active imagination is the method by which the alchemical transformation is instigated and fueled.

In this symbolic picture, we see many details that signify various elements that contribute to and play a role in this coming process. The Sun and Moon in the upper left and right corners are symbolic representations of the main figures in the theater piece, a King and a Queen. Psychologically, they represent the animus and the anima, respectively. From the Mercurial fountain's three spouts flows an abundance of water, which collects in the basin and constitutes the essential catalytic medium for the pair's union and transformation. The water symbolizes Mercurius, the fluid ingredient needed for the process of alchemical transformation and union. Psychologically understood, this is the transcendent function, the linking function between conscious and unconscious. Without this fluid, the two elements cannot be brought into intimate contact with one another, which is required for their mutual transformation and union.

Mercurial water is the solvent and the catalyst for the process. The inscription on the rim of the basin states that the Mercurial water flows from three sources: as "virgin's milk" (a

65

feminine source), as "spring of vinegar" (a masculine source), and as "water of life" (a mysterious and transcendent third source). This is the thrice-great Mercurius. In alchemy, it was said that Mercurius is the beginning and the end of the process. Almost invisible, this mysterious agent makes possible the union of the distinct and separate members of the couple. Mercurius is a metaphor for the largely unconscious psychological "field" in which the mystery of transformation takes place. Mercurius, himself androgenous and therefore a union of animus and anima, represents the invisible hand of the self, which is ultimately responsible for "the mystery of individuation."

Picture 2: "King Sol and Queen Luna"

In the second picture of the series, the protagonists in this dramatic story, King Sol and Queen Luna, appear in full regalia. Initially, they meet both dressed in their royal garments. They meet as apparent equals with equivalent, albeit different, standpoints. King Sol represents the splendor of solar consciousness. As the animus, he represents the archetype of spirit, the ruler of the visible world and its collective consciousness. His power and authority lie in his matchless will and brilliant rationality — rationality in the sense of Nous. He meets Queen Luna robed in his official symbols of office. He wears red garments. Similarly, Queen Luna is dressed in her official capacity as ruler of the Lunar world. She wears white. Hers is the realm of dreams and imagination and emotion. It is a magical realm of subtle connections through unconscious attachment and projection. She favors the body and its instincts as opposed to the spirit and the intellectual mind. As shown here, they are not beginners with potential for growth in stature and identity before them but rather fully articulated archetypal powers. It is a meeting of archetypes.

Here we see the animus and the anima in all their official glory and commanding authority and now meeting in a friendly but quite formal fashion. Their regalia suggests an initial defensiveness in this encounter, clad in their respective armors of persona. But they are in tactile contact with their left hands, a gesture that suggests their forthcoming intimacy. With their right hands, they offer red and white flowers emblematic of their contrasting natures. The left-handed contact reveals the already existing unconscious intimacy between them, which is at this point a potential for a more explicit relationship, while the right-handed offering is a more conscious introductory gesture. Secretly, they are brother and sister, and this is a reunion of two who were once one. Jung speaks of theirs as an incestuous relationship that is reserved for "royalty." As animus and anima, they were once two aspects of a syzygy when they were in the womb of the self. Later, they became separated and developed independently, and now they are coming together again. We are witnessing the beginning of a potential integration in a mature personality.

In the heavens above the two figures is a star, and below it is a dove holding a branch in its beak that reaches down to their crossed branches. This symbolizes a spiritual blessing for this meeting. A Holy Spirit presides over their union as the *spiritus rector*. The picture tells us that Mercurius supports the process that is unfolding. The meeting is auspicious. The dove functions like the Holy Spirit at a ceremonial wedding.

From an intrapsychic perspective, this picture shows the individual's readiness to enter into an engagement with the unconscious. Typically, this is done through active imagination. In order for this to have the optimal result of full integration of the opposites, both sides need to meet as equals. When this is the case, a dialogue can begin, which will lead to the next stage of the union between them.

Picture 3: "The Naked Truth"

The third image shows King Sol and Queen Luna disrobed. They have removed their official wrappings and are now meeting one another fully exposed and without persona identities between them. Trust has been established,

and this encounter is becoming serious. The figures are no longer holding left hands as in the former scene, where the intimate relationship between them was only suggested; now it is explicit. With their right hands, they hold the flower that symbolizes their nature, and with their left hands, they receive the gift of the other. And the dove still hovers above them, indicating its continuing support of the process and its blessing.

Exchanging words for the first time, they indicate that they have a conscious understanding and acceptance of what is happening between them. This is the evidence that the transcendent function is in place and active. Conscious and unconscious are prepared to unite. It is proposal of marriage: "Oh, Luna let me be thy husband," says King Sol. Queen Luna accepts his proposal with the words: "Oh, Sol, I must submit to thee." The dove above them declares itself to be "The Unifying Spirit."

We want to reflect for a moment on what it means to strip away the personas of King Sol and Queen Luna. The Queen, who represents the anima side of the syzygy, loves her attachments — to the body, to beautiful objects, and to other people. She finds her identity in these relationships. The King, who represents the animus side, prefers critical detachment, objectivity, and the exercise of will and superior power over his surroundings. He tends to identify with ideas and concepts in the collective atmosphere, and he finds his identity in these abstractions. These elements compose their personas. In order to join each other in a genuine union, both must put the persona aside. They must become naked, without history. The soul (anima) must liberate herself from her attachments to others and to the material world of beautiful objects and sensual pleasures and must now focus her desire for attachment on the spirit (animus). The spirit (animus) must liberate himself from his former attachments to collective opinions and the "will to power" and focus his desire on the soul (anima). In short, they must enter an entirely new space devoid of other commitments. It is the beginning of something radically new.

This was Jung's move when he left "the spirit of the times" and followed "the spirit of the depths" as he writes in *Liber Novus*. Otherwise, it would not have been a new (*novus*) book (*liber*). This shedding of previous attainments (persona) and attachments (loved objects), whether material (body, beauty, possessions) or cultural (opinions, ideas, concepts), is the condition for entering into this possibility for union of soul and spirit, anima and animus. It means facing the truth about oneself with naked honesty. It requires shedding the past in order to transform into a new being. This is often the midlife crisis experience: burying the past, entering into liminality for a time, and finding a way to the integration of anima and animus.

In the first half of life, the main psychological task is to come into the world and get into life. The newborn has to be seduced into life and become attached — first to the mother and father, then to wider family and friends, then to peer groups and to the culture around and about. It's essential that the anima (soul) enter into life, become active in the world, and get emotionally connected to familiar things and people, or the person will not survive the difficulties of existence. Similarly, it is important for the animus (spirit) to develop the will, to take charge of decisions that matter in life, to develop a standpoint that fits in with the spirit of the times, the cultural norms and values of the surrounding society. This is the role of educational institutions. Traditionally, women have chosen the anima-dominant course, and men have chosen the animus-dominant one.

All of this is developmentally important, and therapists are trained to help their clients do this necessary work of attachment and adaptation. But upon entering into the second half of life, in order for a united mentality (*unio mentalis*) to develop, a separation of anima from favored attachments and animus from identifications with persona and ideals needs to take place. The soul, as the alchemist Gerhard Dorn wrote, has to be separated from the body and united with the spirit.[3] And the spirit must turn away from identification with ideology

---

[3] For Jung's discussion of Dorn's stages, see *Mysterium Coniunctionis*, *CW* 14, Chapter VI.

and bend toward soul. The way the alchemists imagined and described this is contained in their writings and drawings. For a period of time, there is a wrenching and difficult process called *separatio*. Imagery of cemeteries and death is emblematic of this state of consciousness. This is what takes place in the midlife crisis. There is a severe loss of meaning and consequent animus disorientation; emotional life becomes confused, and the anima disappears and is absent for a period of time. It's a difficult passage, but when it's done well, a new perspective opens up. This liberation from previous attainments frees the mind from its shackles and bondage to the past. This is where we are in Picture 3 of the Rosarium. King Sol and Queen Luna have put aside their past and are now ready to embark on a new life together. This picture concludes the preparation for the transformations to come.

With Picture 4, the process of union (*coniunctio*) begins.

The preliminaries over, the two naked figures, both still wearing their crowns to signify the bare residue of their identities as King Sol and Queen Luna, animus and anima, are seated in the Mercurial bath. The water is a solvent that will remove any remaining resistances to their union. The Mercurial water is also the catalyst that will change the outcome of the process from being a mere mixture of separate qualities to a compound, which is a new substance. This picture signals that the process of transformation will be effective. Their meeting is blessed as before by the presence of the Dove, i.e., the support of the Self.

This leads immediately to Picture 5, "The Conjunctio."

Here we see a graphic image of King and Queen floating on the water in a conjugal embrace, having intercourse and approaching the moment of symbolic union. They now speak to one another for the first time:

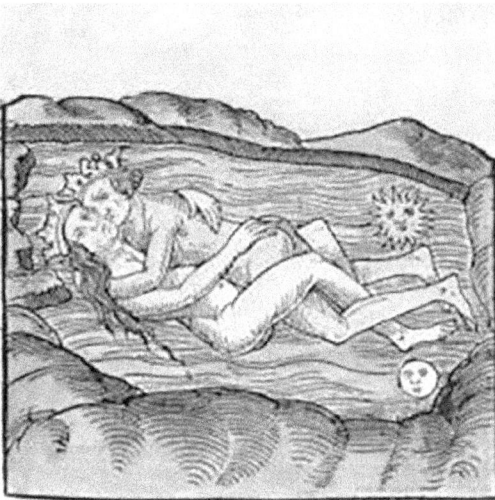

Oh Luna, folded in my sweet embrace,
Be you as strong as I, as fair of face.
Oh Sol, brightest of all lights known to
men,
And yet you need me as the cock the
hen.

King Sol and Queen Luna are reflecting each other's high value. He is giving her his brilliant light, and she both admires him and reminds him that he needs her instinctually, as the cock needs the hen. They belong together spiritually and physically. It is notable that Queen Luna brings in the language of animal instinct. Instinct is the force that brings about union of the pair. Solar consciousness is not self-sufficient, as Luna reminds Sol.

In Picture 6, we see the result of their union. This is the first of three deaths in the *Rosarium* Series.

This picture is titled "Conception" or "Putrefaction." The two figures have become one, and the text accompanying the picture reads:

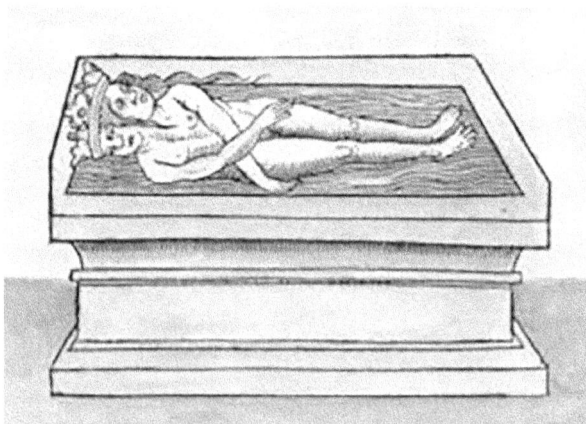

Here lie the King and Queen dead.

The Soul is separated with great grief.

The nigredo state has been achieved. In paradoxical celebration of this moment in the process, the alchemist Arnoldus cried out: "When thou see thy matter to wax black, then rejoice because it is the beginning of the work."[4] For this reason, corruption (death) is also conception (a new beginning). Death of the old must precede the birth of new life. It's the death of the sharp opposition and separation between animus and anima, which is at the same time in preparation for a new state of consciousness. In this picture, we see for the first time in the Series a conjoined figure bearing two heads with one trunk, two arms, and two legs. The image of two heads suggests some continuing differentiation, but since both rely on a single body, they must be together in an altogether new way. This is the inauguration of a New Being, and the figure will continue as such to the end of this part of the series. The goal of union has been achieved, but the resulting body is in a coffin, thus in a liminal state of fusion. To all appearances, the figure is dead.

Psychological liminality is what one experiences during major transitional periods in the individuation process, such as midlife and old age, when a previous identity has collapsed but a new identity has not yet emerged. It is a chrysalis stage, which the alchemists referred to as *nigredo*.

In Picture 7, we see the newborn soul that has been conceived by the royal couple flying upward into the heavens. The conjoined body is left behind, now temporarily soulless. Liminality deepens.

---

[4] The Rosary of the Philosophers, p. 41.

This picture is titled "The Extraction or Impregnation of the Soul." On the one hand, the newly created soul is being extracted from the dead body; on the other hand, the soul is entering into a process of impregnation to be prepared for a new life. The soul flies upward into the heavens where it will dwell for a period of time in the pregnancy. The picture shows us the starting point of incubation. The soul is to grow quietly in the clouds. The text reads:

> Here the four elements are separated,
> And the soul is most subtly separated
> from the body.

The four elements — air, fire, water and earth — had previously been united in the separate bodies of the two protagonists to form solid identities. Now, these identities have dissolved, and a state of *solutio* prevails. Both have died to their previous identities, and in this period of liminality, they are waiting for a new consciousness to be born. The state of incubation in the chrysalis stage continues in this dissolution of solidities. At this point, animus and anima are no longer identifiable. There are no images and no thoughts in this dead body.

Picture 8, titled "Washing," or "Mundification," signals the cooperation of the heavens in preparation for the new state of consciousness. In this phase of the *Rosarium* Series, it is primarily the Queen who is being prepared for the further transformation of the united couple. The water that is falling on the two-headed corpse is not ordinary rainwater but a special elixir with Mercurial properties. It is what Arnoldus calls a "philosophic moistness which is fit for your work ... in which the metallic essence dwells."[5]

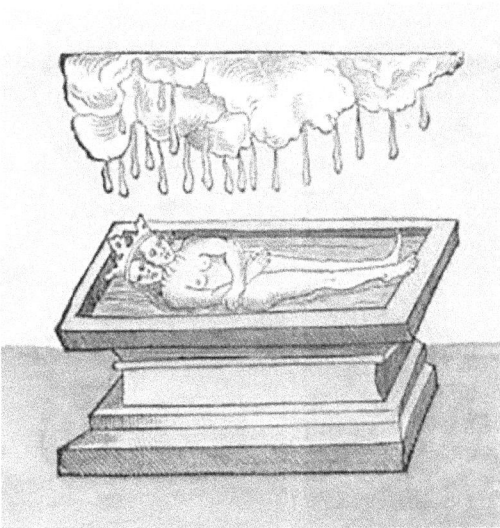

---

[5] *The Rosary of the Philosophers*, p. 53.

The alchemists would speak of this as the *albedo* stage, the stage of whitening. The darkness of night's *nigredo* gives way to the light of dawn. One can also think of springtime, when plants begin to show new life after the deadness of winter. The moisture that is falling on the dead body will bring new life. The text reads:

Here the dew falleth from heaven,

And washeth the black body in the sepulchre.

The "dew from heaven" is a reference to the biblical story of Moses and the Chosen People wandering in the wilderness and being nourished by the Lord with manna, which was a kind of gummy resin that arrived with the dew of the night.[6] Here it is used to purify the body of the couple lying in a tomb. It is therefore transcendent and related to the spirit of the Lord, which "was carried upon the waters before the creation of heaven and earth."[7] Washing with "philosophic moisture" has the effect of reducing the power of traumatic memories and resultant complexes that block further psychological development and create emotional stagnation. One recalls the poet Dante bathing in the river Lethe at the end of *Purgatorio*.[8] This is basically the work we do in analysis with the assistance of the self. The cleansing effects of the therapeutic relationship are supplemented and strengthened by the use of active imagination. The alchemists would call this latter procedure *meditatio*,[9] a conversation with imaginal figures. This is necessary in preparation for the new attitude that is made possible by the union of animus

---

[6] Numbers 11:9.
[7] *The Rosary of the Philosophers.*, p. 54.
[8] See Chapter Two, above.
[9] See C.G. Jung, *Psychology and Alchemy*, *CW* 12, para. 390.

and anima. The revival of the dead body depends on being bathed in this philosophic water. The dead body must be purified in preparation for rebirth. This is an essential task to be undertaken during this period of liminality.

Picture 9, titled "Of the Rejoicing or Springing or Sublimation of the Soul," shows the return of the soul from the heavenly clouds.

This will initiate the rebirth of the body, which means the ability to act in the social and material world in a new way. The text reads:

Here the soul descends from on high,
And revives the putrefied body.

Rebirth is immanent, but it is not yet complete. This is the first of three rebirths in the series.

At the bottom of the picture, we see two ravens, one buried with just its head sticking out of the earth, the other standing free. They seem to look longingly at one another. It is as though they are a pair like the royal couple, but they are not yet able to fly free. As the soul descends from above, the ravens emerge from below. The project is not fulfilled, but it is well underway. In fact, it is almost halfway to its goal, which is fully achieved later in Picture 20 after two more deaths and rebirths. It is a long and slow process.

Picture 10 is a kind of preliminary apotheosis. This is the Lunar Rebis. Standing on the crescent moon, the resurrected body of the united pair is now standing upright, strong and alive. It is a dramatic display, a first version of the New Being.

The Rebis ("from the Latin *res bina*, meaning dual or double matter"[10]) is a symbol of the New Being as a union of soul and spirit, anima and animus. The androgenous nature of this being is on full display: one body with two heads, both crowned, King and Queen in a single figure. Neither eclipses the other. Both are represented equally, Sol looking to the right, Luna to the left. In this Picture we see the reunited Syzygy triumphant.

The fact that they are standing on the moon signals that this is "the Lunar Rebis;" the accent is given the anima side of the Syzygy. This first set of transformations has to do with the transformation of the anima. The second set will have to do with the transformation of the animus. The figure

---

[10] https://en.wikipedia.org/wiki/Rebis

in this picture is somewhat more feminine than masculine, although the masculine is also represented by the head of King Sol on the right side of the body. The text reads:

> Here is born a rich and noble Queen
> Whom the wise men liken unto their daughter.
> She increaseth and bringeth forth infinite children.

The Lunar Rebis represents the transformation of the Queen, who has now incorporated into her body the consciousness of King Sol alongside her feminine lunar consciousness. This brings about the emergence of an incredibly fertile and creative energy within the anima archetype. This is what poets like Goethe, Blake and Maria Rainer Rilke wait for — a *femme inspiritix* to stimulate their poetic genius. The ancients called her a Muse. She brings intuitions and dreams that inspire the imagination, motivating acts of spontaneous creativity. In the Bible, she is named Sophia, the playful figure who was with the Lord God when He created the world and all its creatures.

Psychologically, this picture indicates that the anima has successfully separated from previous attachments to objects in the material world and is now united with the animus. She has been liberated and transformed by her new relationship to spirit. Soul and spirit exist now in a state of unity. In conscious life, this brings an attitude of objectivity and freedom from emotions and obsessions about everyday life in the immediate world. It does not mean uncaring or indifference, but rather freedom from domination by unconscious complexes that obsess and control our emotional and mental life. It is a spiritualized state of mind, as indicated by the wings on the back of the Rebis figure. It is also strong, as we see in the outstretched arms holding serpents in their competent hands.

This is the conclusion of the first phase of the transformation process. It results in what the alchemists called the White Stone.

With Picture 11, the second major phase of the unification of King Sol and Queen Luna begins, which result in the "Red Stone." In a sense, it repeats the previous transformation process, but this time it has to with the transformation of King Sol primarily and takes place on a more spiritual level, as indicated by the wings on the figures. This will be the transformation of the mind (animus) as the previous sequence showed the transformation of the soul (anima).

The text reads:
Here Sol is again included
And is circumpassed with the Mercury of the
Philosophers.

"The Mercury of the Philosophers" is plainly a symbol representing the active presence of the spirit of the unconscious, Mercurius.

In this set of seven images, beginning with Picture 11 and continuing through Picture 17, King Sol undergoes a process of transformation similar to what Queen Luna underwent in the previous set of seven pictures. This is the second conjunction, and while it bears a resemblance to the previous one, there are some significant differences. In this first picture, the transformed and winged Queen Luna is in the upper position with King Sol beneath her. This reversal signals the mutuality of influence that each is having on the other. Neither is dominant, neither installed as the leader. Both are in this together. It is a dialogue. Both figures are winged now, indicating a spiritually advanced state of consciousness at this point.

This second union takes place, therefore, on a level that is less instinctually driven and more conscious than the first. The process has moved to another level. The archetypal element is more prominent in this phase. This is because Sol is related to the world of spirit as Luna is to the body, the world of materia. Archetypal images shade over into the realm of spirit, as Jung writes, as instinctual impulses shade into the world of the body.[11] At both ends of the psychic spectrum there is a psychoid region in which psyche gives links to a realm beyond its boundaries. In the first phase, anima was removed, or released, from her bondage to the body, its impulses and instincts; with this next set of transformations, animus will be released from the control of cultural and archetypal conditioning. The animus, now brought into the center of the process, will undergo a transformation engendered by Mercurius, the spirit of the unconscious and the agent of transformation. This will be a "philosophical" transformation. The animus will be affected at the level of ideas. Ideas are archetypal elements, which exist on a psychological plane with archetypal images. The "philosophical mind" is an archetypal mind, a mind that is in contact with the world of the archetypes. We can think of it as a Platonic mind rather than an Empirical mind. It is what the Greeks called *nous* (νοῦς) the archetypal basis of mind itself.

---

[11] C.G. Jung, "On the Nature of the Psyche," *CW* 8, para. 417.

Although the picture presents us with an image of erotic physicality, the wings on the figures stress the symbolic nature of the union. This is based, it should be said, on the earlier transformation that has already taken place. The physical has been "taken up" or "sublimated" into the realm of spirit, which is where this present transformation is about to take place. The transformation of the animus takes place at this level of psycho-spiritual reality. The mental background by which the psyche operates in its thinking, beliefs, and cultural attitudes will be scrubbed clean and remade.

Picture 12, titled "Illumination," is a death scene, parallel to Picture 6, and there ensues from here a series of pictures in which the corpse of the Androgyne is again featured.

In this picture, you see the shining head of winged King Sol resting on a tomb. The text reads:

>Here Sol dies again,
>and is drowned with the Mercury of the Philosophers.

Again, the "Mercury of the Philosophers" is mentioned, and this is the reason the picture is titled "Illumination." This is a moment when Sol descends into the darkness of the grave. There he experiences the "light of the darkness" and becomes what the alchemists called *"Sol niger,"* the "black sun." It is the night sea journey of the Sun god, Re, so well-known in Egyptian myth. This is a moment in the transformation process when the light of solar consciousness is extinguished so the paradoxical light of the darkness may be perceived. It is a different type of consciousness from the solar, an "illumination" from the unconscious depths. This is what spells of depression can teach us about the deeper meaning of life.

The next picture, 13, which is also set in the tomb, is titled "Nourishment." Thus this seeming "death" is looked upon as a positive development.

The alchemists would say, "Rejoice when you arrive at the nigredo! The process is underway!" Depression is seen as an important part of transformation. The text for Picture 13 reads:

>Here Sol is made black like unto pitch,
>With the Mercury of the Philosophers.

This is *Sol niger.* It is a state of depression, emotionally speaking, but also an experience of enlightenment. This experience paradoxically nourishes the spirit. It adds the dimension of depth. It inaugurates what we call "depth

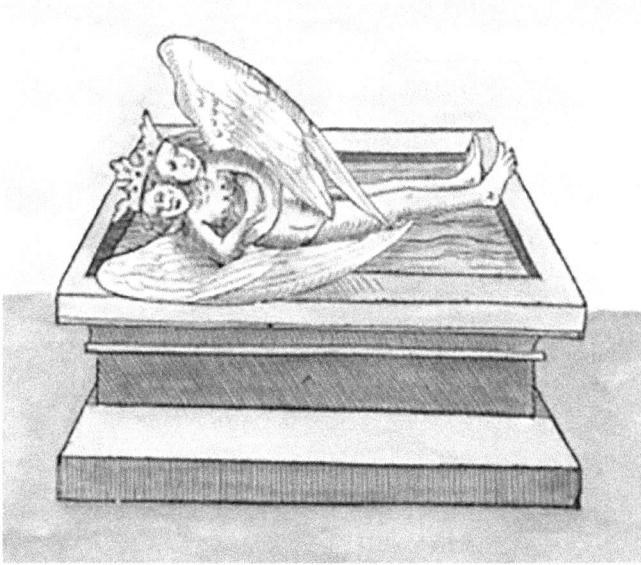

psychology," a vision of life from the perspective of the grave. The surface of life looks shallow by comparison. The animus, which as an archetype underlies the solar mind and therefore ego-consciousness, becomes routinely contaminated by what Jung called "the spirit of the times." Consciousness gets filled with collective opinions and views, some of them noble and high-minded. These accoutrements are fed into the unconscious background (i.e., the animus), and they need to be washed away. Much of our education is a process of filling our minds with the thoughts of the past and of the present cultural consensus, instilling collective attitudes, biases, and prejudices. When we say that someone is "animus possessed" (be it man or woman), this is what we are referring to. These notions are what we think of under the guise of being "rational," and we cannot get out of this collective mentality as long as we travel in these

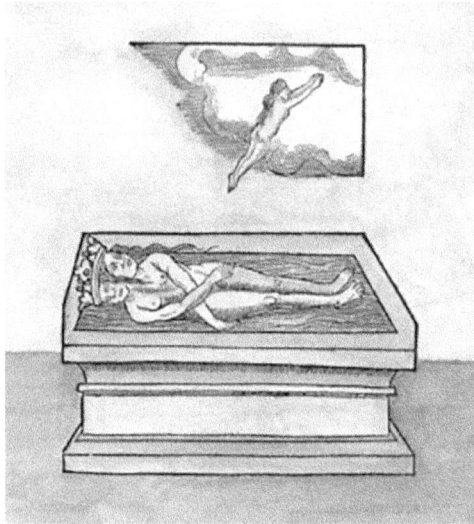

well-trodden ruts. The animus needs to become separated and purified of these extraneous collections of ideas and thoughts that diminish its spiritual light. What the *Rosarium* is showing us is a radical process of separation from material and spiritual attachments that keep us from the truth of the Self. As we will see in the last pictures, the process does arrive at a state of total transformation.

In Picture 14, titled "Fixation," the united pair appears again, but now stripped of their wings. The spirit has left them and is flying upward into the heavens.

The text reads:

Here ends the life of Luna,

And the Spirit subtly ascends on high.

In Picture 7, the matching image from the previous series, we find the soul leaving the body behind. Here the situation is somewhat different: The anima (Soul, Luna) is dead and the animus (Spirit) is leaving for the transcendent heavens, its invisible homeland. In this frame, total silence and darkness prevail. Both anima and animus are absent. It is the *novilunium*, the darkest phase in the lunar cycle and generally considered to be a time of danger. The text declares, however, that this is a time for "fixation," which means stabilization. In the meantime, there is no movement, not even on the cellular or molecular level. The neurons are quiet. It is the Void: no sensations, no thoughts, no images. The Spirit, which has departed, is flying upward for advanced exposure to the Divine realm of transcendence. It will return later, and vigorously, but for now all is silence. A new identity is forming, and the ground for it needs to be "fixed in place."

Picture 15, titled "Multiplication," mirrors Picture 8 ("Washing") and signals the preparation for the return of the flown spirit.

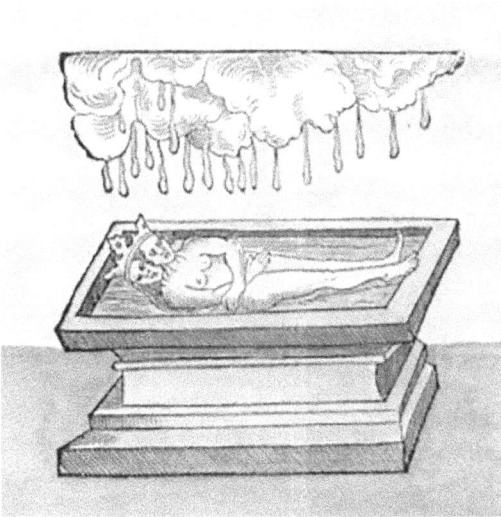

The androgynous figure lies quietly in the tomb and receives the fertilizing rain from above. It is a picture of approaching reawakening of life as in the Springtime. The second round of transformation is nearing completion. The text reads:

> Here water is diminished,
> And bedeweth the earth with his
> moisture.

The "waters of life" are washing the body of the dead body ("earth") in preparation for the second rebirth. This is equivalent to Dante's drinking of the waters of the river Eunoë, which strengthened the virtues of his solar consciousness in preparation for his entry into Paradise.[12]

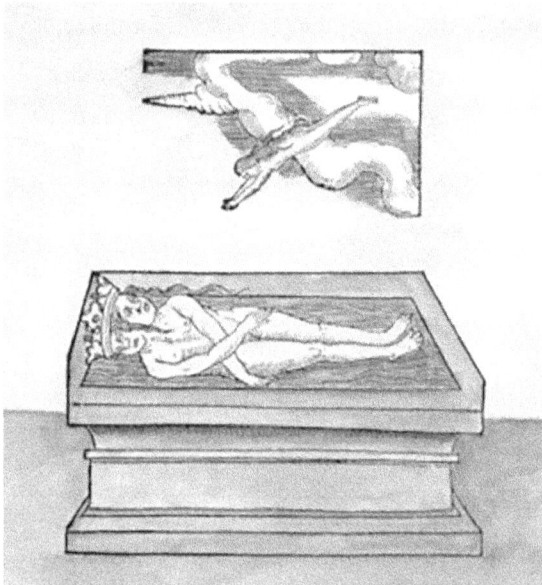

---

[12] See Chapter Two, above.

Picture 16 shows the return of the soul, which had departed earlier for a sojourn in the clouds above. This is a telling image because the returning spirit is now quite mature in comparison to the one that left earlier. She is now strong and clearly intent on reentering the lifeless body in the grave. One thinks of the song, "Morning has broken, like the first morning ..." The image is about to break into celebration, as we shall see in the next picture. The text reads:

> Here the soul descendeth gloriously
> from heaven,
> And raiseth up the Daughter of
> Philosophy.

Aurora is on the horizon. Queen Luna, who died in Picture 14, will be reborn as "the Daughter of Philosophy," that is, as a spiritualized anima, the anima united with the animus. Her orientation has been completely changed. And the animus is now woven into her identity, intimately and permanently.

In Picture 17, we behold the triumphant culmination of this second phase of the transformation process, the Solar Rebis, also known as the Red Stone.

This is in a sense the complement of "the Lunar Rebis" ("the White Stone") in Picture 10. The Solar Rebis, however, is more commanding and robust, and so is more than a mere complementary statement. The image is much more complete and developed, more whole, more powerful. By comparison, the first Rebis was pale and bloodless, as the moon is in contrast to the sun. This picture represents the alchemical *rubedo*, when the brilliance of alchemical gold makes its sudden appearance. The text for this picture reads:

> Here is born the King of all glory.
> There cannot be any created
> Greater in the world than he,
> Neither by art nor nature.

It is surprising that the series does not conclude here. The sun has risen, King Sol is reborn and integrated with Queen Luna. Both now have a place in an integrated consciousness. The image looks perfect and complete, anima and animus successfully integrated and on the same level. Is this not the peak and summit of psychological and spiritual development? Animus and anima are combined in a single image: The lion (solar power and Logos) and the serpents (lunar instinct and Eros) and the self-sacrificing pelican (love) are all contained and united in one symbol. But there is still one more stage of development to go, and again it involves death and rebirth.

This third and final passage through death and rebirth, which begins with Picture 18 and concludes with Picture 20, is so mystical and employs imagery that so strongly suggests the afterlife that I am inclined to think of it as a stage of individuation that exceeds this life and extends into the Beyond. It brings to mind, also, a poignant question raised regularly by elderly and aging clients who are beginning to notice some mental decline and infirmity, who ask: If I should (God forbid!) descend into dementia as I age further, will all that I have gained by way of inner work and individuation in my life just melt away and disappear? Does any of that survive the deterioration of the body's brain or the death of the body? I will interpret this last stage of transformation as shown in the *Rosarium philosophorum* as a partial answer to those questions. Alternatively, one may consider this to be an exceptionally advanced and rare stage of the individuation process experienced already in this life.

Picture 18 is the third death scene in the *Rosarium* series. A Green Lion, representing Mercurius, is devouring the Sun.

The Sun, which represents the previously attained stage of psychological development, doesn't appear happy to be getting devoured by Mercurius, and blood is flowing. This is the ultimate baptism by immersion in the Mercurial waters. The integrated personality is being swallowed up by the collective unconscious, and it will disappear from view in a way and to an extent that the conjoined Sun and Moon, dead as they were in the grave, did not. The Lion announces:

> "I am the true green and golden lion
> without cares,
> In me all the secrets of the Philosophers
> are hidden."

Mercurius, the spirit of the unconscious, claims that in his belly lies the mysterious Gnosis ("all the secrets of the Philosophers") long sought after by the Adept. To get there, it is necessary to suffer this descent into death. Only with this deep knowledge of the very foundation of the psyche, the alchemists believed, could they gain the power to transform other materials, to turn base metals into gold, to cure all illnesses and heal all wounds, and to gain immortality. In the belly of the Green Lion lie the secrets that are contained in the mind of God. This is the wisdom of the transcendent Self. Of Mercurius, Jung writes in *Mysterium Coniunctionis*: "Mercurius demonstrably corresponds to the cosmic Nous of the classical philosophers. The human mind is a derivative of this and so, likewise is the diurnal life of the psyche, which we

call consciousness."[13] He houses the bottom line of ultimate wisdom.

This as a picture of death symbolizes the most intense introversion, which takes the transforming personality paradoxically into the heavenly realm that we see in the next picture. This shows the divinization of the human: A human being is crowned, signifying a change of identity from personal and historical to archetypal and eternal.

The Holy Trinity is placing a crown on the human figure as the sacred words of a sacramental action are spoken (or sung) in the sky above. This is the crown of glory that would have traditionally, according to Catholic doctrine, been given to the faithful Bride of Christ, the Church. Alchemy

---

[13] C.G. Jung, *Mysterium Coniunctionis*, *CW* 14, para. 117.

unashamedly claimed a comparable reward for those who pursued the opus faithfully to its conclusion.

The ultimate gift to the individuating personality is the elevation of identity to the archetypal basis and fundamental essence of the personality with no residue of the temporal remaining. In a sense, this is the culmination of the previous two ascents of the soul to the heavens above the corpse of the conjoined pair as shown in Pictures 7 and 14. In Picture 19, we see into the Beyond and witness what is happening there. This is the story of Dante's journey into and through the heavenly realms in the third canticle of *The Divine Comedy*, *Paradiso*. There the poet becomes privy to the transcendent realities and mysteries and is, in turn, transformed by his visionary experience as he writes, that he could feel the center of his thoughts and desires being guided "by the Love that moves the Sun and the other stars." He becomes one with Divine Love and is no longer the Dante Alighieri who lived in Florence, endured years of exile, and became a famous romantic poet. Internally, he is Divine, as is his immortal poem.

The theme of divinization is continued in the final picture in the series, the image of the risen and triumphant Christ. This is the third rebirth in the *Rosarium* and takes the series to an entirely new level. A possible reference in the mind of the alchemist might have been the words of Paul in 1 Corinthians 13 promising a destiny like Christ's, which shows the conquest of the power of death itself:

> Behold! I tell you a mystery. We shall not all sleep, but we shall all be changed, in a moment, in the twinkling of an eye, at the last trumpet. For the

trumpet will sound, and the dead will
be raised imperishable, and we shall be
changed. For this perishable body must
put on the imperishable, and this mortal
body must put on immortality. When
the perishable puts on the imperishable,
and the mortal puts on immortality, then
shall come to pass the saying that is
written:

"Death is swallowed up in victory."

"O death, where is your victory?

O death, where is your sting?"[14]

The fear of death is dissolved. The text accompanying the
picture in the *Rosarium* reads:

---

[14] 1 Corinthians 13:51-55.

"After my passion and manifold
torments I am again risen,
Being purified and cleansed from all
spots."

Conclusion

The alchemical transformation process thus goes beyond the union of animus and anima to a direct identification with the Self, in which the ego disappears into a transcendent unity of spirit and matter. This is the ultimate destination of the alchemical process and corresponds to Dorn's third stage of transformation, the union of the fully integrated psychological individual with the *unus mundus*.

The analogy, or identity, of the product of the alchemical transformation mystery to the resurrected Christ caused concern among the Church's theologians, who proceeded to declare alchemy a false and misleading teaching, a heresy. In effect, the alchemists were saying that human individuals could attain to the spiritual level of the transcendent Christ. Jung, following the alchemical masters, speaks of "the Christification of many" in his subversive work, *Answer to Job*.

One must keep in mind as a psychotherapist that this process lends itself to the possibility of archetypal inflation, a danger that Jung discussed earlier in his work "The Relations Between the Ego and the Unconscious," where he refers to the so-called "mana personality." There he writes that the archetypal image "rises out of the dark background and takes possession of the conscious personality entails a psychic danger of a subtle nature, for by inflating the conscious mind it can destroy everything that was gained by coming to terms with the anima." [15] It is a danger not to be minimized, but it can be avoided if the images remain impersonal and related to as aspects of the archetypal psyche. St. Paul's words, "it is no longer I who live, but Christ who lives in me,"[16] show a narrow path between inflation and denial. The "new being" that Paul's theology speaks of is the "Christ within," but this does not abrogate the continuing struggles of the ego with the complexes, pride, and other characterological infirmities.

The *Rosarium Philosophorum* can be considered to be a map of the individuation journey, the psychological state of division and projection to the goal of unity and conscious selfhood. In the course of this journey, the opposites as represented by King and Queen, the images of animus and anima, comes into intimate contact with one another. In the process, too, both are transformed. The animus is cleansed of its notions and accumulated cultural conditioning, and the anima is divested of her previous emotional attachments and dependencies. They become exclusively invested in each another and become one. This constitutes binocular vision, conscious and unconscious in harmonious play with one another to achieve a clear vision of reality inner and outer. The personality shows exquisite psychological balance between action and reception.

Ultimately, there is a birth of transcendence in consciousness that rises above all divisions created by the psyche, and a person enters into a space of supreme Oneness, beyond even the division between time and eternity, where

---

[15] C.G. Jung, "The Relations between the Ego and the Unconscious," *CW* 7, para. 378.
[16] Galatians 2:20.

Samsara and Nirvana are one and the same.[17] In the biblical words of Jesus of Nazareth, "I and the Father are one."[18] These are states of mind beyond all conditioning.

These affirmations state the final goal of individuation. Even if not achieved, they are worthy of consideration as one journeys through life. Meditating on the pictures of the *Rosarium* has been a way for some people to find their way toward this final goal.

---

[17] According to Nagarjuna, an ancient Indian philosopher, "Nothing of Samsara is different from Nirvana, nothing of Nirvana is different from Samsara." Both are products of the temporally bound mind and therefore without ultimate reality.
[18] John 10:30.

"The Piano Lesson": Wolfgang Pauli's Mysterious Union of the Opposites[1]

Wolfgang Pauli's active imagination, "The Piano Lesson," was for him a *mysterium coniunctionis*, a union of "the opposites" as classically described by Jung in his last book.[2] For Pauli, the critical issue was to forge a union between science and depth psychology, causality and synchronicity, rationality and spirituality, anima and animus. This would be expressed symbolically in this active imagination as "piano music." While "The Piano Lesson" is a symbolic drama in the mystery of individuation with specific reference to its author, it also speaks to a possible union of the opposites for postmodern culture in general. As a culture, we still have a long way to go before we have assimilated the message in this profound proposal for a Weltanschauung that will serve adequately for the present and the future.

The notion of synchronicity is the key to Pauli's proposal for a new account of reality. It is deeply embedded in Pauli's active imagination piece under consideration here. This was an insight that preoccupied him for many years, and it grows out of his relationship with Jung. It was also a

---

[1] W. Pauli, Die Klavierstunde. Eine aktive Phantasie über das Unbewusste. In *Der Pauli-Jung Dialog und seine Bedeutung für die moderne Wissenschaft* (eds. H. Armanspacher, H. Primas, E. Wertenschlag-Birkhäuser), pp. 317-330. In English: W. Pauli, "The Piano Lesson," pp. 122-134.

[2] C.G. Jung, *Mysterium Coniunctionis*, *CW* 14.

passionate interest he shared with M.-L. von Franz, Jung's brilliant student and in a sense heir to this theory, which she developed at length in many of her works, particularly in *Number and Time*. These comments are made to set the stage for discussing "The Piano Lesson."

Synchronicity

Today, the term "synchronicity" is familiar and widely used among cultural elites throughout the world. More than that, nearly everyone, if asked, can easily report a synchronistic experience, and many people feel that synchronistic events have changed the course of their lives. People may not have a theory to explain it, but they know what one means by "meaningful coincidences." Such coincidences have been known and recorded since time immemorial. In previous ages, they were seen as divine interventions, as messages from the gods, or as blessings, or sometimes as curses. Since the European Enlightenment and the enshrinement of the Goddess Reason, however, serious scientific thinkers have generally dismissed such coincidences as mere chance events devoid of objective meaning. What meaning can be assigned to them, it is thought, is purely subjective and the product of wishful thinking, superstition, paranoia, or fear. For Jung, however, there was a message in them. He argued that objective meaning could be discovered if looked for, and in his writings, he spoke of them as "acts of creation in time,"[3] thus disrupting the scientific consensus of Jung's time

---

[3] C.G. Jung, "Synchronicity: An Acausal Connecting Principle," *CW* 8.

that causality and the iron laws of nature leave no room for spontaneous acausal creation in the material world.

Wolfgang Pauli, steeped as he was in modern science and its methods, nevertheless worked deeply, intensely, and over a long period of time with Jung on the study of synchronistic phenomena and the implications of synchronicity for modernity. In fact, Jung's major conversation partner on this subject was without any doubt this mathematical genius and Nobel Prize-winning physicist. Both men considered themselves to be scientists, but both were convinced that the modern scientific account of reality was incomplete.

Jung was undoubtedly extremely pleased to have such a brilliant collaborator for this project, which he says began to take root in him as a result of a meeting with Einstein in 1912. To the table Pauli brought his hyperacute thinking, long famous for its sharp-edged thrusts in arguments with his scientific colleagues. Pauli had impressed Einstein already as a youth of 18 when he wrote a detailed review of Einstein's paper on the theory of relativity and its mathematical equations. Both men belonged to the small group of scientists who revolutionized the field of theoretical physics and laid the groundwork for quantum theory and modern cosmology.

It is remarkable that a scientist like Pauli would be drawn to depth psychology. Evidently, the positivistic science practiced and taught in the universities of his day was not enough for Pauli. He had a suppressed religious side to his personality that bordered on the mystical, and Jung's depth psychology turned out to be a way to release it and give it expression. Pauli turned out to be, unconsciously at first, a seeker after meaning and psychological wholeness.

At the beginning of his relationship with Jung in 1933, Pauli was suffering from a severe split in his personality between conscious and unconscious tendencies. The rational-thinking animus ruled entirely, and mystical-feeling anima was entirely absent or only found in projection onto unsuitable women. At the suggestion of his father, a professor of chemistry in Vienna who recognized his son's suffering for what it was, Pauli, a professor at the ETH in Zurich, contacted Dr. Jung for psychological help. Following an initial interview, Jung referred him to a student of his, Dr. Erna Rosenbaum, because he quickly determined that Pauli's problem had to do with the repressed shadow and anima and that it would be better to work this out, at least initially, with a woman analyst. This was brilliant on Jung's part, as the results of Pauli's analysis with Rosenbaum quickly proved. Pauli gave himself to the process without reservation, and from the beginning of his analysis, he recorded his dreams and "waking visions" (active imaginations) with incredible dedication and precision. Analysis opened the door to his unconscious, and he walked through it boldly and without hesitation. He was a "natural" and very gifted explorer into the depths of the unconscious. It was there that he found his missing soul.

From the 400 items in this material, as recorded during his initial eight months of analysis with Rosenbaum and later also with Jung, and Jung's interpretation of a selection of them in *Psychology and Alchemy*, Part II, one can gather that Pauli was a mystic in disguise as a scientist, and very well disguised indeed to the outside world. This is certainly not to take away anything from his brilliance as a mathematician and a scientific thinker but only to give him his due as much more than such accolades might claim.

104

"The Piano Lesson," composed in the fall of 1953, only some five years before his untimely death in 1958, makes clear Pauli's continuing dedication to the search for a way to unite animus and anima and find a trans-binary position. Even this late in his professional life and after 20 years of contact with Jung, he was suffering from the problem of resolving the differences between what he calls "the two schools," quantum physics and depth psychology, and struggling with the question of how to bring them together into a single, unified type of consciousness. This was a central motif in his earlier dreams and vision and later in discussions with Jung as we can see in their correspondence,[4] and it is the burden of "The Piano Lesson." As Pauli puts it in this imaginative work, science offers "words" (of explanation) and psychology offers "the meaning" of those words in the language of image and emotion. How can they be combined in a single language? The symbolic answer to this burning question for Pauli is "piano music," which is made up of sounds from both white and black keys. Animus and anima are married, and causality and synchronicity are brought into a single unified theory. This symbolic marriage takes place in the active imagination Pauli sends to M.-L. von Franz.

As Jung and Pauli worked ever more deeply into the interface between quantum physics and depth psychology, they wrestled with the phenomenon of synchronicity and its implications. For science, the psyche (a realm of image and imagination, conscious and unconscious) and the material world are strictly separated domains. Scientists study the material world to discover its laws, and to do this objectively,

---

[4] C.A. Meier, (ed.) *Atom and Archetype: The Pauli/Jung Letters.*

they try to do everything they can to eliminate psychological factors such as projections, personal and cultural biases, etc., from their research. They want to discover the impersonal, objective laws of nature. Once these laws become known, they can be used to make predictions, to create new technologies, and generally to bring nature under greater human control. The theory of synchronicity, however, purports to bring the two domains, psyche and matter, together under a single complex formula. As generally defined, a synchronistic event is, as Atmanspacher and Fach summarize, "a coincidence phenomenon in which ordinarily unconnected mental and physical states are experienced as connected,"[5] and one should add, "and as *meaningful*." In fact, meaning is the most critical feature of synchronicity.

The theory of synchronicity is a contribution to the understanding of reality, but it is not an easy one to digest and integrate because of the way one normally thinks. The theory asserts that the psyche is deeply entangled with the material world and should not be considered as a second and different realm. It is precisely this entanglement that brings meaning and creativity into play in this "dual-aspect monistic"[6] account of reality. For Pauli, it remained to be worked out how this would look in his life and his work as a professor of physics at the Federal Institute of Technology (ETH) in Zurich.

---

[5] H. Atmanspacher and W. Fach, "Synchronistic mind-matter correlations in therapeutic practice," p. 79.

[6] For a discussion of dual-aspect monism and its place in Jung's and Pauli's thinking, see J. Cambray, "German Romantic Influences on Jung and Pauli," in (ds.) Harald Atmanspacher and Christopher A. Fuchs, *The Pauli-Jung Conjecture*, pp. 49ff.

If the factor of synchronicity in a sense transcends causality, it does not abolish it. Relating these two dimensions and bringing them together into a single unified field theory became the great challenge facing Jung and Pauli. It is comparable to bringing the East and the West into a unified world picture on the one hand, and bringing consciousness and the unconscious together in the realm of psyche on the other. The systems in both cases are incommensurable, as Jung states clearly in a letter to Pauli,[7] and yet they must be brought into a unified whole if a full picture of reality, whether psychic or cosmic, is to be drawn. Similarly, when one consults the *I Ching* with a Western-trained scientific mind, the two incommensurate systems are brought into play, as Jung demonstrates in his brilliant "Foreword to the *I Ching*." In the correspondence between Jung and Pauli, one finds various proposals for how to diagram a world picture that would include both causality and synchronicity.[8] Jung published their final version in his essay "Synchronicity: An Acausal Connecting Principle."[9]

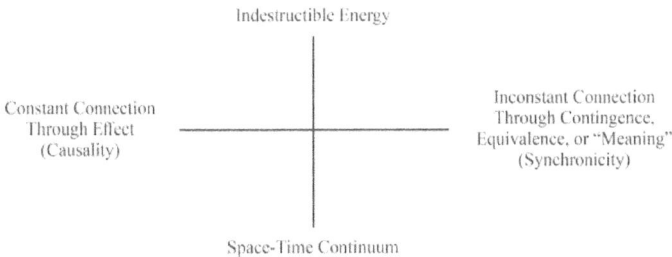

Indestructible Energy

Constant Connection
Through Effect
(Causality)

Inconstant Connection
Through Contingence,
Equivalence, or "Meaning"
(Synchronicity)

Space-Time Continuum

---

[7] C.A. Meier (ed.), *Atom and Archetype*, p. 61.
[8] *Ibid.*, pp. 56-61.
[9] C.G. Jung, "Synchronicity: An Acausal Principle," *CW* 8, para. 963.

What synchronicity introduces into the discussion of chance events like coincidences is "meaning," that is, something transcendent, spiritual, coming from a source beyond any figures featured in the event. Additionally, synchronicity derives from a source that is autonomous and creative, which lies beyond both psyche and matter. It is these three features of synchronicity — the unity of psyche and world, transcendent meaning, and creativity — that challenged the scientific world picture in Jung's time and does so still in ours. Synchronicity theory disrupts our modern way of thinking to such a degree that a scientist like Pauli must have been initially disturbed to the core of his being by it. In "The Piano Lesson," he uses imagination in trying to find a solution to the question of how these two principles — lawful causality on the one hand and synchronicity on the other — can be brought together in a unified world picture.

"The Piano Lesson": An Active Imagination

To understand how Pauli approaches this problem of uniting animus and anima, we need to begin by looking at the method he uses for engaging it, i.e., active imagination. Jung developed active imagination as a method to create what he called a transcendent function, that is, a bridge or connection between ego-consciousness and the unconscious. When successful, active imagination introduces a disruption in normal ego-consciousness in such a way that it is able to step beyond its usual boundaries and enter into a dialogue with unconscious figures and images. As a result, the ego moves into contact with what Erich Neumann called the archetypal field and the self-field.

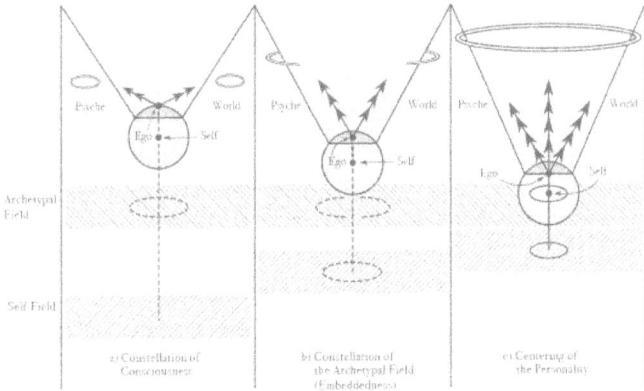

This drawing, which Neumann includes in his Eranos paper "The Psyche and the Transformation of the Reality Planes,"[10] represents the movement that may take place in active imagination. The diagram represents three fields of knowledge: an ego-field, an archetypal-field, and a self-field. There are also three stages, or states, of consciousness, which move in the diagram from left to right: a) Constellation of Consciousness, b) Constellation of the Archetypal Field (Embeddedness), and c) Centering of the Personality. The three stages show different levels of relationship among the fields below the ego level and differing degrees of separation between psyche and world above the ego field. As the stages move from left to right, the three fields come closer, the bottom levels rising. At the top, there are three degrees of separation between psyche and world; moving from left to right, we see this distance closing. Moving from left to right, the bottom rises, and the top closes as the state of consciousness

---

[10] E. Neumann, "The Psyche and the Transformation of the Reality Planes," p. 19.

achieves what Neumann calls "centering of the personality." Our interest is in the movement toward awareness of *unus mundus*, which unites psyche and world.

The stage on the far left represents ego-consciousness, which divides inner subjective and outer objective spaces, and equally divides conscious and unconscious within the inner realm. There is no perceptible connection between them. On an everyday level, most of us live in the state of awareness on the left. Common sense, education, and modern secular attitudes lend their weight to dividing the world and the psyche in this way. Occasionally, we may sense ourselves in the middle stage, when material from the archetypal field impinges on our awareness, as in active imagination. And once in a while, perhaps, we find ourselves in the state of unified consciousness represented on the right, where all the levels and divided worlds unite.

Once the ego is in closer contact with these fields, the gap between psyche and matter begins to close, and a sense of *unus mundus*, i.e., a unified, nonbinary world, emerges. Neumann explains this in detail in a later Eranos paper, "The Experience of the Unitary Reality." This is precisely what we see happening in Pauli's "Piano Lesson":

> I have the impression that the white keys are like the words and the black keys are like the meaning. At times the words are sad and the meaning joyful, then again it is just the other way round. Here, with you, it is no longer as in the two schools which gave me so much trouble: I can always see that there is only *one* piano.[11]

---

[11] W. Pauli, "The Piano Lesson," p. 126.

In this moment, Pauli reaches a position in which the two
schools combine their contributions and a single piece of
music is heard.

"The Piano Lesson" begins with a sudden reversal
of time to a period in Pauli's life when he was a teenager. In
his old home in Vienna, he finds himself in the presence of
an impressive older woman, who is identified as "the piano
teacher." He is here to take a lesson. As we move through
the story, three figures occupy the stage as main characters:
Pauli himself, a female figure or anima who takes a couple
of forms, and the Master, or Self-figure. The female figures
and the Master both have a history in Pauli's earlier dreams
and active imaginations, which I will not detail here.[12] "The
Piano Lesson" becomes a story of establishing solid relations
among these three figures, and this is precisely what occurs in
Neumann's third stage of consciousness. The anima figure, i.e.,
the piano teacher, presents the archetypal field, and the Master,
i.e., the Self-figure, represents the Self-field. When they are all
brought together, Pauli finds that there is no longer any conflict
between the "two schools," and piano playing on both white
and black keys becomes a possibility. What does this mean?

The white keys represent the school of modern science
and mathematics, which uses a "language" for describing
and investigating the relations among material objects from
an objective standpoint. The psyche is excluded as much as
possible from the field. The black keys represent the language
of meaning, the qualitative rather than the quantitative side of
experienced reality. Here, psyche is the essential component
in the investigation. When the two are brought together

---

[12] See H. Van Erkelens and F.W. Wiegel, "Commentary on *The Piano Lesson*."

and music is played with both black and white keys, one hears the music of a unified world where empirical fact and mathematical law and meaning all sound together. Causality and meaning (i.e., synchronicity) unite in a single field. The incommensurables unite in a trans-binary third position, which is represented by the music made by the two sets of keys played together. The white keys do not exclude the black keys, as one finds in the science departments of the universities, as Pauli says; nor do the black keys exclude the white keys as one might find in the theological schools and religious institutions where only meaning resides and tries to dominate over empirical fact and natural laws. This piano music combines them, so one gets the sense of living in a world where science and meaning come together and do not contradict one another but rather where each contributes some notes to the whole.

Pauli's Lecture to the Strangers

In the middle of "The Piano Lesson," surprisingly, Pauli changes to his present age. Still within the active imagination, he is now suddenly called upon to give a lecture to strangers. This comes about when Pauli makes a telling statement about chance. Generally, the idea that nature operates by fixed rules and laws dominates the thinking of scientists. The absolute rule of causality in nature is the result of this principle. In the world of quantum physics, however, the rigid laws of nature seem to be suspended, and probability takes their place. But probability is not secure and can easily bring about disruptive change. This opens the doors to freedom from the laws of nature, but it does not in any way include the element of meaning. Chance can be blind and serve no purpose. At this point in the active imagination, Pauli says: "chance is always fluctuating, but sometimes it fluctuates systematically."[13] It is systematic fluctuation that opens the door to possible meaning.

At this moment, an abrupt change occurs in the active imagination, and Pauli is instructed by the Master to give a lecture to a throng of strangers who appear outside the window. Pauli is now his present age and speaks as a university professor. This will be the inauguration of his new vocational mission, to occupy the chair of quantum physics and depth psychology unified. His lecture is on biology, however, and he argues that evolution is based on two principles: adaptation to environments and chance mutations. The chance mutations can be shown to follow a pattern of systematic fluctuations such that a line of development occurs from simple organisms eventually onward to the emergence of homo sapiens and the human psyche, a creature that is capable of advanced forms of consciousness. This is a development in nature that shows underlying meaningful coincidences taking place all along the way of evolution of life on planet Earth. Pauli points out that mutations often occur before they demonstrate their importance for adaptation to environment, hence they are not responses to environmental pressures but rather originate elsewhere in some source of underlying creativity.

This anomaly in the pattern of mutations brings into play the notion that creativity resides in a location within reality that implies meaning and purpose. A mutation has purpose, even if this cannot be seen at the moment of its appearance in material reality. In other words, synchronicity takes place in

---

[13] W. Pauli, "The Piano Lesson," p. 127.

nature and in history apart from humankind and when humans are not around to recognize it. This is a broader definition of synchronicity than Jung started with, which was restricted to the meaningful coincidence between a content occurring in human psyche and in the external material world at the same time. With the extension of the theory, the natural world quite apart from humanity's participation also shows the principle of synchronicity in operation. First, synchronicity happens, then causality follows, and further developments then show lawful pathways. The two principles work together to bring the world into being. This is piano playing, or what van Erkelens calls "symphonicity."

After Pauli's lecture to the strangers gathered outside his window, the anima figure cries out: "I think you have given me a child." [14] ("Ich glaube, du hast mir ein Kind gemacht.") Apparently, his lecture has brought about a *coniunctio* and generated an offspring, which represents the union of animus and anima and the consequent production of a "third thing," or unified trans-binary position. This is a further symbolic expression of union of the opposites in "The Piano Lesson," a parallel to the piano playing that unites the action of both black and white keys to produce music.

"The Ring *i*"

"The Piano Lesson" concludes with a highly symbolic scene in which the anima figure removes a ring from her finger, which Pauli had not noticed until then. The ring symbolizes the union between Pauli and the woman who has just born him a child, and it is designated as "the ring *i*."

---

[14] *Ibid.*, p. 134.

The symbol "*i*" speaks in the language of mathematics. It is an "imaginary unit" that opens up new dimensions within mathematical fields. With this symbol, "complex numbers" can be created, which combine real and imaginary numbers. The symbol *i* is a sort of magical unifier of the opposites, in alchemy known as Mercurius. "The *i* makes the void and the unit into a couple,"[15] Pauli says to the woman. (This is a union of unconscious (the void) and ego-consciousness.) To which the woman replies: "It makes the instinctive or impulsive, the intellectual or rational, the spiritual or supernatural ... into a unified or monadic whole that the numbers without the *i* cannot represent."[16] In other words, it unifies all levels of being, material, psychological/mental, and spiritual. Here it is presented in the form of a very special kind of wedding ring: "It is the marriage and at the same time the realm of the middle, which you can never reach alone but only in pairs."[17] This announces that the goal of arriving at and living permanently in the realms of wholeness has been achieved. Animus and anima are united. The "ring *i*" is the symbol of their irrational and eternal bond, now consummated.

This consummation is then impressively affirmed by "the voice of the Master," who "speaks, transformed, from the center of the ring to the lady: 'Remain gracious.'"[18] This is a direct reference to the apotheosis of Faust in the closing stanzas of Goethe's poem, where Doctor Marianus speaks the lines addressed to Mater Gloriosa, the Eternal Feminine:

---

[15] *Ibid.*
[16] *Ibid.*
[17] *Ibid.*
[18] *Ibid.*

> *Jungfrau, Mutter, Königin,*
> *Göttin, bleibe gnädig!*
> Virgin, Mother, Queen,
> Goddess, remain gracious!

It is a prayer for the future and a blessing for the union between Pauli and the anima figure who has offered him "the ring *i*" and borne a child with him. The Eternal Feminine is invoked by the Master, and this prayer, which is also a blessing of the permanent union between animus and anima, means that she is now freed to assume an intimate conscious relationship with the protagonist. The *mysterium coniunctionis* has taken place.

The Piano Lesson

The Lysis of the Story

This would be the end of a fairy tale, but it is not quite the end of "The Piano Lesson." After hearing the blessing from the Master, Pauli suddenly finds himself out of the framework of the fantasy and back in normal time and space, i.e., no longer in the ego-archetypal-self constellation as described by Neumann as the third stage, but rather back to the first. In other words, the active imagination is over, and the normal state of ego-consciousness returns. Now Pauli is again wearing his usual coat and tie and goes about his business as a science professor. As he walks away, he hears the woman at the piano. She plays a C-major chord of four notes C E G C. This sequence is a quaternity symbol and corresponds to the famous saying of the alchemist Marie Prophetessa: "Out of the one comes the two; out of the two comes the three; and out of the three comes the one as the fourth." This affirmative major chord signals a sense of completion and a successful culmination of this lesson at the piano, and because Pauli can still hear her play, albeit at a distance, it means that their relationship remains intact. A significant transformation has taken place within Pauli's psychic matrix.

An Open Question

A question remains, however, about how to understand this ending. It is normal to return to one's usual ego-consciousness and identity following an intense active imagination. However, some commentators like Herbert Van Erkelens and M.-L. von Franz have taken this ending to mean that Pauli abandoned his commission. He promised to return to the home of the piano teacher and has been given

117

a new vocation to teach about the harmonious interface of physics and psychology, but he reneges on his promises. He never returns, he never carries this purposeful mission into the world of his profession, and he simply closes the lesson and forgets about it. This is their harsh judgment, but I do not find it persuasive.

It is clear that the marriage has effectively taken place on an inner level. Pauli has forged a permanent and transformative bond with the anima. This is meant for his own private purposes, however, and not for the outer world of his professional or social life. The inner marriage of animus and anima may have been reflected in some subtle ways in his behavior and relationships, but it was not made explicit in his lectures or publications. It was a private mystical experience that was meant for him alone, although he shared it with M.-L. von Franz and indeed dedicated it to her, but otherwise, he kept it private as a carefully guarded secret. My intuition tells me that he continued to play the piano for himself; that he continued to hear the music of causality and synchronicity combined throughout the remainder of his life. This would mean that he did indeed continue to see the events in his life, from the largest to smallest, as meaningful and that he kept a watchful eye out for new acts of creation in time.

But perhaps this was music for a future age, and that age would be ours. It is then left for us to nurture and raise the child born to Pauli and the Lady in "The Piano Lesson." One might take this beginning further, as Jung and Pauli suggested and Neumann and von Franz did in their own time. More recently, Atmanspacher and Fach have proposed a structural-phenomenological typology of mind-matter correlations. I will not go further into this fruitful development here but rather only confirm that this work is being done presently by a variety of people and at a sophisticated intellectual level. Clinical applications of this correlation theory have been taken up by Joseph Cambray, Angela Connolly, and Yvonne Smith Klitsner.

Conclusion

The other day in Zurich I saw a sign in front of a sweets shop: "A Day without Chocolate is like Champagne without Bubbles." Yes, I thought: That would be "flat." Now it occurs to me that a world ruled by causality alone and without synchronicity is like Champagne without Bubbles — "flat." Imagine a life without meaningful coincidences that turn you in an entirely new direction; a world in which everything is completely and rigidly predicable; a world without creativity and surprise, without disruption, without the beautiful possibility of a chance encounter with a stranger that turns out to be transformative for your life. This would indeed be Champagne without bubbles.

Thank goodness we do not live in such a world.

Mysterium Coniunctionis: "The Mystery of Individuation"[1]

In 1955, the year of Jung's 80th gala birthday celebration in Zurich and of the publication of his last book, *Mysterium Coniunctionis*, Joseph Campbell published a collection of papers titled *The Mysteries*. This had been the theme of the Eranos Conference held during World War II in 1944. The volume consists of 13 lectures by such outstanding figures in Religious Studies as Walter Otto, Karl Kerényi, Walter Wili, Hugo Rahner, and, of course, by the lone psychologist among them, C.G. Jung. "Mystery" seems to have been a topic of general interest in 1955, and it was certainly close to Jung's heart and mind.

Mysterium grew out of Jung's decades-long study of alchemy, but not only from that source. Other and perhaps more important sources of inspiration were his own personal experiences in active imagination, which resulted in the now-famous *Red Book*, *Liber Novus*, and his work as a psychotherapist, a doctor of souls. If one takes a look at his analytic praxis room, partially hidden as it was behind his library and resembling a sacred space (a *temenos*), replete with symbolic objects and stained-glass windows from an old medieval church, one has the distinct feeling that it was a kind of magical chamber where the mysteries of psychological

---

[1] This phrase is from Jung's *Black Books*, vol. 7, p. 227.

transformation were practiced. His essay "On the Psychology of the Transference," published in 1944 as a preliminary work to *Mysterium*, is a brilliant account of the hidden mysteries of transformation as they play out in the therapeutic relationship. For good reason, he had earlier called the "fourth stage" of analysis nothing less than "transformation."[2] This was the mystery: psychological transformation. The transformation was always "uncanny" and, as he would often point out, "synchronistic," i.e., coming about *Deo concedente* ("God willing"), by seeming accident. The entire process of individuation at its deepest level was a "mystery," beyond predictability and rational explanation.

Jung further argued that there was an undeniable resemblance between modern psychotherapeutic treatment and the practices and outcomes of the ancient mystery religions. The ancient Mysteries consisted of rites of initiation into the respective cults, while at the same time instigating psychological and spiritual transformations that would strongly affect an initiate's entire life. They effectively activated and advanced individuation processes in the depths of the unconscious, always, of course, *Deo concedente*. The Mysteries included various rites that induced altered states of consciousness in the prospective initiates with the purpose of offering them a numinous experience of "the ineffable." As Jung argues, this was an experience of "the living presence of a numinous archetype."[3]

The most famous of these were the Eleusinian Mysteries. In this cult, which was located near Athens

---

[2] C.G. Jung, "Problems of Modern Psychotherapy," *CW* 16, para. 160ff.
[3] C.G. Jung, *Mysterium Coniunctionis*, para. 312.

and dedicated to the goddesses Demeter and Persephone, the initiates were taken down into the darkness of a cave where they encountered the presence of the goddesses. The experience was *arreton* ("unutterable"[4]) and therefore would necessarily remain secret. Its transformative power depended on this ineffable experience. In its 1,500 years of existence as an active cult, the rites of the Eleusinian Mysteries were never disclosed by the initiates to any outsiders. In part, this is because the initiates were sworn to silence, but another reason was that they *could not* talk about it. It was beyond their powers of articulation. Certain experiences in analysis are like this as well: *arreton*. Clinical reports are normally flat and prosaic, but the experience inside the temenos of treatment may be ineffable.

The Mysteries of Isis were of a similar nature. The only even partial testimony to what happened there is found in the picaresque novel *Metamorphoses (The Golden Ass)* by Apuleius, in the concluding chapter, where the author offers a brief glimpse into the secret rites practiced by the priests and experienced there by the initiates.

While Jungian methods of analysis might resemble the mystery religions of ancient times in some ways, Jung did not, contrary to rumors, found a cult, meaning by that a closed society with secret rites and rituals of initiation. In their professional societies and institutes, Jungian psychoanalysts do not as a group engage in cultic practices as, for example, the Masons do. Nevertheless, there is an aura of the secret and the sacred in the analytic space. Analysis is committed to strict confidentiality, and it has a powerful transformative

---

[4] K. Kerényi, "The Mysteries of the Kabeiroi," p. 37.

effect on the participants due to their strong engagement with the unconscious. At times, they do touch upon "the living presence of a numinous archetype." This is an essential aspect of the individuation process as it is engaged in analysis. And it does have the emotional quality of "a time filled with sacred events and having a specific atmosphere," which we speak of as a "field." The notion of a psychological field is taken from electromagnetics, and when applied to the interpersonal interactive space between analyst and analysand, it speaks of the conscious and unconscious connections that become activated and generate psychic energy sufficient to induce transformations.

Because of their transformative power, the "mysteries" of many cultures and religions fascinated Jung. The numerous references to "mysteries," "mysterium," "mysticism" and the many other related topics in the index of the *Collected Works* testify to his long-standing interest in this topic. His extensive research into the mystery of transformation was certainly not meant to acquire a token to pass entry into "the spirit of the times," where it would have a negative value for the most part anyway; nor was it undertaken for only purely personal reasons, of which there were plenty, as we shall see. It was rather driven by his discovery of a striking resonance between such ancient practices and the psychological transformations that he witnessed in himself and in his consulting room as a practicing psychoanalyst. There was something archetypal, i.e., universal, about this process of psychological transformation that he named "individuation," and he was intent on exposing it to the light of modern consciousness.

For Jung, the word "mystery" would immediately suggest "the unconscious." Phenomena are mysterious because our consciousness cannot encompass them or grasp their meaning. Their cause is unknown or opaque and hidden from our view, at least at the moment. As such, they attract unconscious projections and become symbolic. The psyche uses its resources to establish a connection to them by projection — of attributes, invisible causes, and imaginative explanations. This provides a kind of understanding, but it is not a scientific one based on exact measurement and evidence of causality. In an Editorial Note for the second edition of *Mysterium Coniunctionis,* Jung writes that in the work he is "concerned with psychological facts on the borderline of the knowable."[5] Not only are these psychological facts unknown at the time; they may be largely unknowable in principle because they are not subject to scientific study in the usual sense of the word. Science may never explain them. Some phenomena are beyond the reach of the rational mind to understand even if they can be described in detail. This, he states, makes it necessary to use metaphors and images to explore this unconscious territory. His method of interpretation would be amplification, the collection of parallel images from other cultures and times.

In fact, the strong use of metaphor and symbol in an explanatory text signals that the subject under discussion is at the "borderline of the knowable" and therefore necessarily carries with it the aura of mystery. Throughout his life, and most dramatically and personally in *Liber Novus,* Jung was given to exploring the boundaries of the known and the

---

[5] C.G. Jung, Editorial Note, *Mysterium Coniunctionis,* p. vii.

knowable, i.e., the unconscious. The multitude of references in the *Index* of the *Collected Works*, to "mysteries," "mysterium," "mysticism" and related topics testifies to the consistent interest Jung took as a depth psychologist in symbolic statements and systems. His paramount mission in life was to explore the unconscious, i.e., mystery.

Alchemy was for Jung, especially in the works of his later years, the most significant of the mystery schools for psychology, but it was far from the only one. Others of major interest were Kabbalah, Mithraism, the Mystery religions of ancient Greece and Rome, and modern esotericisms. His extensive research into the Mysteries of many religions and mythologies amounted to depth psychological research into the unconscious foundations of structures and processes that lie beneath the surface of personal psychological and collective cultural constructions. Jung had from the beginning of his career sought to look beneath and behind the surface of the flux of phenomena as registered by the senses in conscious life to perceive the invisible psychological and spiritual forces that shape them. As he understood his mission, the task of depth psychology was to investigate the dynamics and the direction of unconscious processes, in other words, the "mysteries," of the psyche. His method was phenomenological: He would study the visible in an attempt to have a look into the invisible background dynamics they all had in common. These he would then call archetypal.

One of the prime archetypal tendencies of the psyche that he discovered is to instigate unification of "opposites" once they have been constellated and set up in the psyche. This is the "*mysterium coniunctionis*" ("the mystery of union") that Jung is writing about in his final book. It is akin to studying the force of gravity, for gravity, too, is invisible and extremely difficult to pin down theoretically and experimentally. Gravity consists in the action of gravitons, but what are "gravitons"? Are they waves or particles? Or both? Jung's question to the psyche was: How can we understand this type of uniting psychological energy ("libido"), which attracts the opposites and pulls them together? As a psychological force, this mysterious gravity-like energy is a key to the individuation process. It is an organizing force that produces a unique and whole personality. From his comparative studies, Jung conjectured that this force is archetypal, i.e., universal, and has a critically important role in the inner and mostly quiet and hidden process of psychological transformation by which the scattered and numerous pieces of psyche become united. *Mysterium Coniunctionis* would be his last and greatest attempt to study this process of unification.

A related issue that I will consider in this reflection is the ancient problem of "the many and the one," i.e., the paradox of diversity and unity, as it pertains to individuation, personal and collective. Does the force that presses for unity conflict fatally with the force that presses equally for diversity and plurality? Or are they complementary pressures that balance one another and can both be accommodated in a single design?

The Red Book Experiment — *Liber Novus*

The classic mysteries show a distinct model for achieving the transformation process. They are invariably based on the archetypal pattern of death-and-rebirth. With this in mind, I will recount Jung's story, as told in Jung's Red Book, titled *Liber Novus*. Jung began his "experiment" (as he called it) in active imagination in November 1913, when he was 38 years old. It became a formative psychological transformation experience that shaped the rest of his life, which at the time was just entering its second half. Quite early in this experiment, he encountered two figures who named themselves Elijah and Salome. Both would play a decisive role in his transformation. The account of this encounter begins in Chapter 9 of *Liber Novus* titled "Mysterium: Encounter" and continues through Chapters 10 ("Instruction") and 11 ("Resolution"). This story marks the climax in *Liber Primus*, the first section of *The Red Book*. These chapters closely follow the pattern we find in the Eleusinian Mysteries and the Mysteries of Isis: preparation, instruction, initiation. Jung clearly recognized this similarity as acknowledged in a note to the text titled "Guiding Reflections": "This my friend, is a mystery play in which the spirit of the depths cast me. I had recognized the conception, and therefore the spirit of the depths allowed me to participate in the underworld ceremonies, which were supposed to instruct me about the God's intentions and works. Through these rituals I was supposed to be initiated into the mysteries of redemption."[6]

Jung is prepared in various ways by Elijah and Salome for the mystery of transformation. At a critical moment in his encounter with them, he receives a teaching (Chapter 10, "Instruction") that will utterly transform his attitude toward the imaginal figures he is encountering and teach him about what he would later call "the reality of the psyche." Here is the conversation:

> Elijah: "You may call us symbols for
> the same reason that you can also call

---

[6] C.G. Jung, *The Red Book*, Reader's Edition, p. 178, ftn. 162.

> your fellow men symbols, if you wish
> to. But we are just as real as your fellow
> men. You invalidate nothing and solve
> nothing by calling us symbols."
> I: "You plunge me into a terrible
> confusion. Do you wish to be real?"
> Elijah: "We are certainly what you
> call real. Here we are, and you have to
> accept us. The choice is yours."[7]

This remarkable declaration by Elijah, which would become bedrock in Jung's theory of the psyche in his later writings, is followed by a dramatic initiation, which is described in Chapter 11, "Resolution." Jung has been carefully prepared for this moment by the prophet and his feminine companion (Jung would upon reflection interpret them as Logos and Eros, also as Animus and Anima). At the critical moment, which will mark the climax of this section of *Liber Novus*, he finds himself caught up in a vision and involuntarily changed by the mysterious power of transformation. He writes:

> I am seized with fear at what I see. ... I
> see the cross and Christ on it in his last
> hour and torment — at the foot of the
> cross the black serpent coils itself — it
> has wound itself around my feet — I am
> held fast and I spread my arms wide.
> Salome draws near. The serpent has
> wound itself around my whole body,
> and my countenance is that of a lion.

---

[7] *Ibid.*, p. 187.

Salome says, "Mary was the mother of Christ, do you understand?"

> I: "I see that a terrible and incomprehensible power forces me to imitate the Lord in his final torment. But how can I presume to call Mary my mother?"
> Salome: "You are Christ."
> It is as if I stood alone on a high mountain with stiff outstretched arms. The serpent squeezes my body in its terrible coils and the blood streams from my body, spilling down the mountainside... The serpent falls from my body and lies languidly on the ground. I stride over it and kneel at the feet of the prophet, whose form shines like a flame.
> Elijah: "Your work is fulfilled here. Other things will come. Seek untiringly and above all write exactly what you see."[8]

Years later in a seminar given in 1925 to his students in Zurich, Jung tells them: "The animal face which I felt mine transformed into was the famous [Deus] Leontocephalus of the Mithraic mysteries."[9] Jung goes on in that seminar to compare his experience with the ancient mysteries:

> These images have so much reality that they recommend themselves, and such extraordinary meaning that one is

---

[8] *Ibid.*, pp. 197-98.
[9] C.G. Jung, *Analytical Psychology*, p. 106.

> caught. They form part of the ancient
> mysteries; in fact it is such fantasies
> that made the mysteries. Compare the
> mysteries of Isis as told in Apuleius,
> with the initiation and deification of
> the initiate. ...One gets a peculiar
> feeling from being put through such an
> initiation. ... In this deification mystery
> you make yourself into the vessel and
> are a vessel of creation in which the
> opposites reconcile.[10]

Clearly, Jung's experience is a modern version of the ancient mysteries of transformation. His experience of "divinization" transformed the anima figure, Salome, and restored her sight, and it took Jung out of temporality and into the realm of the gods, into eternity. The Mithraic god, Aion, presides over time and specifically over the astrological revolutions and is thus beyond temporality and its limitations.

A related issue in *Liber Novus* arises repeatedly around the problem of love. Throughout *Liber Novus*, Jung struggles with the meaning of love. As we know, for Dante the ultimate reality of the universe was Divine Love, and for him, this was represented by Christ. In *The Divine Comedy*, the final result of the ultimate revelation in the last Canto is described as follows:

> Yet, as I wished, the truth I wished for
> came
> Cleaving my mind in a great flash of
> light.

---

[10] *Ibid.*

> Here my powers rest from their high
> fantasy,
> But already I feel my being turned —
> Instinct and intellect balanced equally
>
> as in a wheel whose motion nothing jars —
> by the Love that moves the Sun and the
> other stars.[11]

Dante becomes one with Love, the divine energy that subsists in the Unus Mundus and is the Prime Mover in the cosmos. In Jung's terminology, this would constitute union with the energies of the Self. In *Liber Novus*, Jung does not reach this level of transformation, but he does get a foretaste of it. Repeatedly and almost compulsively throughout *Liber Novus*, he reflects on the figure of Christ and the Christlike total commitment to love.

It is noteworthy that Jung's calligraphic transcription from the manuscript for *Liber Novus* into the Red Book ends abruptly in midsentence. It is an astonishing rupture in the text, a moment similar to the flash of lightning that concludes Dante's poem. It occurs just as Jung is about to receive a strange gift:

> Bird: "Do you hear me? I'm far off now. Heaven is so far away. Hell is much nearer the earth. I found something for you, a discarded crown. It lay on a street in the immeasurable space of Heaven, a golden crown."
> And now it already lies in ... (here the

---

[11] Dante, *The Divine Comedy, Paradiso* XXXIII: 140-146.

calligraphic text ends)
What Bird deposits in Jung's hand as a gift is "a golden crown, with lettering incised within; what does it say? 'Love never ends.' A gift from Heaven. But what does it mean?"[12] Jung is puzzled by the gift.

From our perspective as contemporary readers of *Liber Novus*, we know that it means Jung is destined to experience a mystery of transformation similar to Dante's. This future is further suggested in the last scene of "Scrutinies," the third section of *Liber Novus*, when Christ makes an appearance in Jung's garden and is recognized by Philemon as "truly a king. Your crimson is blood, your ermine is snow from the eternal cold of the poles, your crown is the heavenly body of the sun, which you bear on your head."[13] A dialogue ensues between Philemon and Christ in which Christ recognizes Philemon as Simon Magus, the ancient magician of biblical notoriety, who has taken this altered form in *Liber Novus*. Philemon tells Christ that he and his wife, Baucis, now play host to the gods, as did the ancient Greek couple. It seems Philemon has extended his identity from the magician to include that of the humble man who with his wife welcomes divine figures into his home. In *Liber Novus,* he is both characters. Philemon declares that a "prior guest" was received in the garden, and it was "your terrible worm," i.e., Satan, the archetypal Shadow figure whom Jesus rejected and who here is recognized as the brother of Christ. Philemon continues: "Now that I gave the worm a place in my garden, you came to me."[14] The worm

---

[12] C.G. Jung, *The Red Book*, Reader's Edition, p. 441.
[13] C.G. Jung, *The Black Books*, vol. 6, p. 245.
[14] *Ibid.*, p. 246.

brought the gift of "ugliness," Philemon declares, and he asks Christ if he has brought the gift of "beauty." Christ replies: "I bring you the beauty of suffering. That is what is needed by whoever hosts the worm."[15]

Suffering the conflict between this pair of opposites will be the path to the next stages in the mystery of transformation for Jung, and this will be a major theme in his last book, *Mysterium Coniunctionis*.

Some three decades later, in the winter of 1944, Jung takes part in another experience of the union of opposites, this time between the masculine and feminine aspects of the Self, as he is recovering from a heart attack in a hospital bed. In a series of three visions, he witnesses the mystic marriages of Malchuth and Tifereth, Hera and Zeus, and Christ and his Bride. In *Memories, Dreams, Reflections*, he gives full expression to his sense of the numinous nature of these visions in words that echo Dante's descriptions of Heaven in *Paradiso*. Jung says: "These were ineffable states of joy. Angels were present, and light."[16] He will later give a full psychological and theoretical account of the meaning of these visions in his masterpiece, *Mysterium Coniunctionis*.

One curious detail about Jung's *Black Book* entry of the scene in the garden with Philemon and Christ is worth mentioning. *Liber Novus* is based on the entries Jung made in his journals called "the black books" as he was having the experiences. In the now-published *Black Books*, the entry for the garden scene is dated 6.VI.16. The entries in the *Black Books* continue with further entries from later dates, but it is

---

[15] C.G. Jung, *Liber Novus*, p. 553.
[16] C.G. Jung, *Memories, Dreams, Reflections*, p. 294.

this entry on June 6, 1916, that is the basis for the conclusion of *Scrutinies*, the third and final section of *Liber Novus,* as it was composed in the manuscript version. In other words, this entry in which Christ appears in Jung's (Philemon's) garden signifies "The End" of *Liber Novus*. The curious fact is that the end of Jung's life falls on the same day of the same month, June 6. The year of his death in 1961 is a number that reverses the last two numbers of the *Black Book* entry date, 1916. Both were Tuesdays, or in German *Dienstag*, meaning a workday (*Dienst* = work; T*ag* = day) of work — or "in service." For Jung, June 6, 1916, was the beginning of his Great Work that would continue until his final day of service, June 6, 1961. The date falls in the astrological month of Gemini, "the twins," a sign that symbolizes the two sides of a single being, symbolic of conscious and unconscious. I present these strange coincidences as a mystery not to be explained. Jung would call it "synchronicity."

Mysterium Coniunctionis — A Study in the Mystery of Individuation

"This book — my last — was begun more than ten years ago," Jung writes in the Foreword to *Mysterium Coniunctionis,* and it is without question his most difficult book to read and comprehend. Densely packed with references and quotations from alchemy, it quickly stops the modern reader from engaging in the usual habit of speed reading. Unlike most of us, Jung could read alchemy texts in the original languages and assumed (incorrectly) that his readers had an education in the classics similar to his. "To understand alchemy," he commented later, "the knowledge of Latin and Greek was essential. I read hundreds of texts that were not translated and still to this day have not been translated. The ones that had been translated I preferred to read in Latin. They were more intelligible to me in Latin."[17] Fortunately for most of us, the English translation of *Mysterium* puts the quotations from alchemy texts into the vernacular. The originals are included in an appendix for those who have a classics education.

Beyond the problem of navigating among those numerous stumbling blocks, the final destination of *Mysterium* is beset by so many detours and byways, albeit fascinating ones, that the reader is often frustrated and left bewildered and lost. The path to the work's final goal, which is to bring the reader to an understanding of what the union of opposites means psychologically, is not straightforward despite the clarity of the Table of Contents. According to James Heisig, this structure furnished nothing but "a sort of mold into which he could empty his files on alchemical literature."[18] In my view, this would be the opinion of a student who had not spent enough time with the text, but on the surface level, it does have merit. The text is extremely intertwined and subtly woven out of many threads from the alchemical literature. In this sense, it resembles the alchemical works Jung is using. Jung has created, in a way, a mirror image of the alchemical writings he was deciphering.

The basic theme of *Mysterium* is fundamental psychological transformation at several levels, conscious and unconscious. To investigate this, Jung chooses to look at alchemy for models of the transformation process. Alchemy

---

[17] A. Jaffé, *Streiflichter zu Leben und Denken C.G. Jungs*, pp. 58-9. My translation.
[18] J. Heisig, *Imago Dei*, p. 108.

was, after all, an attempt to transform the worthless into the valuable, waste material into spiritual gold. Jung draws on the works of major alchemical figures such as Maria Prophetessa, Senior, Geber, Nicholas Flamel, Gerhard Dorn, Valentinus, Raymond Lully, Thomas Norton, Paracelsus, and Abraham Eleasar as well as alchemical texts from the major collections. His private library of alchemical works, which he assembled over several decades, was one of the most extensive in the world at the time.

In addition to this formidable obstacle to a modern person's understanding — Greek and Latin quotations in the original, tangled and intricately connected references to obscure alchemical works, a method of exposition that is more circular than straightforward — the reader has to know quite a lot about Jung's earlier writings in order to grasp this one. This book stands at the apex of a pyramid of writings extending from 1900 to 1955. The publication of *The Red Book* in 2009 and *The Black Books* in 2020, moreover, coming more than 50 years after *Mysterium*, add to the complications because they are now also considered to be essential reading in order to understand *Mysterium* adequately. It is a tall order indeed! Many people give up and put the book back on the shelf, saving it "for later." For myself, having lived with this work for nearly 50 years at this point, I still feel like something of a novice explorer poking around in a vast field of hidden gems of psychological wisdom. The word "mysterium" is not out of place! And I confess, it is my favorite of all of Jung's books.

We have to regard this late work in the context of the author's history, personal and intellectual. *Mysterium* is much more than an academic summary of Jung's decades-long intensive studies of Western alchemical writings. It

137

is a profound penetration into the mysterious processes of psychological and spiritual transformation that are inscribed in these obscure, almost undecipherable, texts and demonstrates, albeit indirectly, how they have a bearing on individuation today. Basically, *Mysterium* is Jung's final word on individuation in its furthest reaches of human possibility. It is about the human potential for psychological wholeness and the path to its realization.

Mysterium Coniunctionis is the only volume in the *Collected Works* whose title is not translated into the vernacular language either in the original German or in any of the many translations. Like the Latin language itself, it stands as a monument to the universal and timeless. The title gives this weighty work an archetypal quality; it has a mystical aura about it that is instigated by the title itself.

The Birth of *Mysterium*: Karl Kerényi and Goethe's *Faust*

In the Introduction, Jung writes that *Mysterium* was initially inspired by Karl Kerényi's monograph *Das Ägäische Fest* ("The Aegean Festival"). First published in 1941, Kerényi's slim work is characteristically brilliant. It is a poetic reflection on a scene from Goethe's *Faust Part Two* that is set in the mythological territory of ancient Greece, the author's specialty. A renowned scholar of Greek mythology, Kerényi was at the time a regular participant in the Eranos Conferences and an esteemed colleague and friend of Jung's. It was no doubt because this scene in *Faust* is set in the imaginal space of mythological Greece that Kerényi took a special interest in it, and it is because there is a strong alchemical element in it that Jung's interest was so strongly drawn to Kerényi's monograph.[19]

Part Two of *Faust* is manifestly symbolic in nature throughout. Unlike Part One, which takes place in the sensible world and is a first-half-of-life story concerning the protagonist, *Faust*, Part Two is set entirely in an imaginal realm of archetypal images and symbolic events. Goethe considered the totality of *Faust* to be an account of his own inner life, and Part Two pertains to his experiences and active imaginations in the second half of his life. Like Dante, he completed his *magnum opus* only shortly before his death. Part Two of the work can be read as a poetic summary of Goethe's psychological and spiritual journey in the late stages of individuation, as he delves into the collective unconscious and discovers the source of archetypal transformation and redemption in what he calls "the Eternal Feminine."

What must have especially captured Jung's attention in the episode that Kerényi writes about is the dramatic appearance of the famous alchemical figure, Homunculus, and the dramatic scene of his *coniunctio* with the beautiful Galatea. In the story, Homunculus was created in Faust's laboratory by the professor's assistant, Wagner, and when we meet the "little man" in this scene set on the Aegean coast, he is eagerly looking for a way to become incarnated as a full human being. He is still enclosed in the womblike alchemical vessel in which he was begotten, and he wants desperately to break out and enter into life fully and materially. When he sees the breathtakingly beautiful Galatea floating offshore

---

[19] For an excellent discussion of alchemical themes in *Faust*, see *A Most Mysterious Union: The Role of Alchemy in Goethe's Faust*, by Stephen Y. Wilkerson.

on a seashell, he becomes electrified and begins to shine. He enlists the help of a nearby philosopher who throws him into the sea, and off he goes in hot pursuit of his love. As his state of excitement increases in her proximity, he glows more and more brilliantly, and at the climax of their encounter, the intensity of his energy bursts his glass bubble, and the two lustily make the waters boil in the frenzy of their passionate *coniunctio*. Witnessing this incredible scene, the onlooking Sirens sing:

> What fiery wonder transfigures the sea?
> The waves splinter and glitter, what
> storm can this be?
> All shining and swaying, a progress of
> light,
> Those bodies aglow as they move
> through the night,
> And the whirl of the fire all about and
> around!
> Now let Eros, first cause of all, reign
> and be crowned!
>> Hail to the sea, the shifting
>> tide,
>> By sacred fire beautified!
>> Hail to the waves, hail to the
>> flame,
>> Hail, this event without a name![20]

According to Jung, this scene "is based on *The Chymical Wedding of Christian Rosencreutz*, itself a product of the

---

[20] Goethe, *Faust*, Part Two, p. 123.

traditional hierosgamos symbolism of alchemy."[21] The scene from *Faust* is a dramatic example of a *mysterium coniunctionis,* and it impressed itself deeply in Jung's mind. As a result, he set about writing what would become his major work on alchemical symbols and individuation.

Kerényi concludes his commentary on the Aegean Festival by writing pithily: "*Homunculus' Abenteuer ist das Mysterium des Entstehens*" ("Homunculus' adventure is the Mystery of Becoming" — or "Emergence," or "New Beginning").[22] A passionate love affair marks the beginning of the mystery of the transformation that will follow: It plants the seed for the next stage of individuation.

In Goethe's poem, this further development will include Faust's imaginal love affair with the divine Helena, the archetypal anima figure of classical Greek culture, with whom he produces a precocious miracle child, the boy Euphorion ("Euphoria"), who flies too high and too far and crashes dead at their feet, whereupon Helena leaves and returns to her life in the realm of the Dead. In the end and at the ripe old age of 100, Faust's soul, upon being released and separated from his body by "eternal love" ("*die ewige Liebe*"),[23] is taken up into Heaven, where the Chorus Mysticus sings:

> All that is transitory
> is precisely [only] a likeness.
> What cannot be attained,
> Here it takes place.
> What cannot be described,
> Here it is done.

---

[21] C.G. Jung, *Mysterium Coniunctionis*, p. xiii.
[22] K. Kerényi, *Das Ägäische Fest*, p. 74.
[23] Goethe, *Faust* II, 11964.

The Eternal Feminine
Draws us up, on and on.[24]
This is the conclusion of Goethe's *Faust* and not so dissimilar
from Dante's in *The Divine Comedy*.

Mysterium Coniunctionis — The Text

Mysterium Coniunctionis is a long, intricately woven,
and artfully constructed book. The Table of Contents is
useful as a quick initial orientation to this most challenging
of Jung's writings. There are six chapters in *Mysterium*: 1)
The Components of the Coniunctio; 2) The Paradoxa; 3) The
Personification of the Opposites; 4) Rex and Regina; 5) Adam
and Eve; 6) The Conjunction. To summarize them briefly:

Chapter 1 sets the stage. Here Jung names the
components in a number of "pairs of opposites" that alchemy
deals with: moist-dry, heaven-earth, fire-water, active-passive,
spirit-matter, masculine-feminine, etc. There are many images
and concepts for this oppositional phenomenon and for their
union, and Jung states that the union is often symbolized by a
quaternity made up of two pairs of opposites. Most frequently,
however, the *mysterium coniunctionis* will feature a cast of
two figures, a male-female pair. The story of their union is a
drama that includes the archetypal death-and-rebirth event as
part of the *coniunctio*. Jung writes that it is "the moral task of
alchemy to bring the feminine, maternal background of the
masculine psyche, seething with passions, into harmony with
the principle of the spirit — truly a labour of Hercules!"[25] For
the feminine psyche, it might be considered "truly a labour

---

[24] Translation kindly offered by Paul Bishop.
[25] C.G. Jung, *Mysterium Coniunctionis*, para. 35.

of Psyche," as in the story of Amour and Psyche told in *The Golden Ass of Apuleius* and interpreted by Erich Neumann.

Chapter 2 introduces the idea of "paradox" as central in alchemy. These are concepts and images, often bizarre, of the union of opposites. An example is the two-headed Rebis. The androgyne is a favored image. Paradoxes attempt to combine the opposites in such a way as to suggest a hidden, underlying unity, as stated in this alchemical quotation cited by Jung: "Why speak ye of the manifold matter? The substance of natural things is one, and of one nature that which conquers all."[26] Regarding the human personality, this underlying unity is the self. Definitions of the self must therefore be paradoxical because the personality is made up of a number of pairs of opposites: persona/shadow, anima/animus, time-bound/timeless, etc.

Chapters 3, 4 and 5 consist of a detailed discussion of masculine and feminine symbols (Sun and Moon, King and Queen, Adam and Eve) and their separate transformations. The transformations are basically about the processes that effect fundamental changes in consciousness, individual and collective (Sun, King, Adam), and in the unconscious (Moon, Queen, Eve). These transformations are preparatory for the unification possibilities that will follow.

Chapter 6 concludes the book and is the most straightforward section and therefore the easiest to follow. In it, Jung presents a psychological interpretation of the alchemist Gerhard Dorn's formula for a three-stage process that transforms consciousness and takes it to an all-inclusive dimension. I will discuss this in more detail later.

---

[26] *Ibid.*, para. 36.

The reason the opposites are such a psychological problem is that they reflect the divided psyche. This splitting apart of the psyche is the result of a normal process of differentiation that takes place in the course of psychological development, individual and collective. It is the result of the birth and growth of ego-consciousness within the original natal self. Ego-consciousness, moreover, is by its nature a separating and differentiating function in the human personality. Without its continuous operation, humans would not be the individual conscious beings they are. The first half of life is largely devoted to this development — separation/ differentiation of the ego from the unconscious and of the individual from physical and social surroundings. This creation of a unique sense of individuality (ego-hood) and identity (persona) is the goal of individuation in the first half of life. From this position, the individual can successfully participate in society as a responsible and self-aware member of the larger collective.

But this development swings a two-edged sword. On the one hand, it offers great benefits; on the other, it creates enormous problems — conflict between oneself and others, neurosis due to repression and one-sidedness, feelings of isolation. The opposites, which are generated out of a preconscious matrix of the original self, introduce conflict. This happens on an individual level and on a cultural level. Original unconscious oneness breaks up into a division, which then is driven toward a regained but now more conscious unity.

In *Mysterium,* Jung works with "opposites" derived from alchemy. They are basically masculine/feminine pairs — Sun/Moon, King/Queen, and Adam/Eve (Chapters 3,4,5)

— whose union is symbolized in images like the androgenous Rebis. Jung often quotes the axiom of Maria Prophetess as a summary of the process: "One becomes two, two becomes three, and out of the third comes the one as the fourth."

In psychology, we observe this process in the course of development as a portion of the original self breaks away and becomes a personal identity centered by ego-consciousness. The features of the personality that are left out of this identity form a shadow identity made of rejected pieces of the self (the shameful or "bad") and the gender part of the original syzygy (animus/anima unity) that were left out of the conscious identity. Individual identity depends on this development. Then, in later life, the problem becomes how to reunite the separated parts of the self. How this may come about is a fundamental question addressed in *Mysterium*. It is a matter of reuniting the divided self.

Another part of the division that opens in the psyche is between the instinctual body and the idealistic spirit. Freud wrote about this as a conflict between the id and the superego and assigned the civilized person's chronic malaise to this dilemma in his *Civilization and Its Discontents*. Jung takes another and more optimistic view of this conflict between instinct and spirit and sees it as soluble, but he recognizes it as fundamental as well. Both sides of the divide must be transformed before a lasting union can come about. This process of transformation is analyzed in chapters 3, 4 and 5 of *Mysterium*.

In Chapter 3, the chief actors are Sun and Moon, the former representing the spiritual/cultural structures of the psyche (solar consciousness) and the latter the cycles and rhythms of the somatic unconscious (lunar consciousness).

145

Much of the chapter dwells on the transformations in the lunar realm (anima). Chapter 4 features the figures King and Queen, a social pair of opposites among the archetypal images of the collective unconscious, and here the principal focus is on the transformation of the masculine/patriarchal dominant of consciousness (animus) with the feminine/matriarchal (anima) in a secondary position. In Chapter 5, the argument is that Adam represents the original Anthropos (wholeness of the self) that falls into division, which results in the constellation of the pair Adam (ego-consciousness) and Eve (the unconscious). The feminine/unconscious aspect (anima, instinct), as represented by Eve and her surrogate, the black Shulamite, is subjected to an intense process of cleansing and transformation whereby she is prepared for union with the similarly transformed male partner, which brings into being Adam Kadmon, a representation of the original self now as reborn.

The Title of *Mysterium Coniunctionis*

The title of the book, *Mysterium Coniunctionis*, should be considered in some detail. The word *mysterium*, as we saw, refers to secret rites and rituals and to sacramental elements in religious practices. The reference to the religious, therefore, is placed strongly and directly into the title of the book. The title suggests, therefore, that Jung is going to speak about mysteries that invoke the powers of the Divine and draw the presence of the transcendent Being(s) into the human realm. The word *mysterium* implies activities of an invisible power that cannot be fully grasped by human cognition but can be experienced, most obviously in religious contexts. Numinous experiences similar to those described in religious texts may also occur in private moments in the life of the individual and not only in collective settings. *Mysterium* is a word used by Rudolf Otto to speak of the *numinosum* in his famous work of *The Idea of the Holy*: it is, he writes, a *mysterium tremendum et fascinans*.

Because of this network of associations to the word *mysterium*, Jung felt a need to explain his use of religious language in an Editorial Note to the second edition of *Mysterium*:

> ... if I make use of certain expressions that are reminiscent of the language of theology, this is due solely to the poverty of language, and not because I am of the opinion that the subject-matter of theology is the same as that of psychology. Psychology is very definitely not a theology; it is a natural science that seeks to describe experienceable psychic phenomena. In doing so it takes account of the way in which theology conceives and names them, because this hangs together with the phenomenology of the contents under discussion.[27]

As he explains, Jung looks in this work to the language and concepts of theology for an account of the material that he wishes to discuss scientifically, i.e., psychologically. He does not want to be taken for a theologian, however, but will use theology for his psychological investigations. Psychology

---

[27] *Ibid.*

147

will deal with "the mysteries" as experienced phenomena, not as revelations of eternal metaphysical truths. The experience of the *numinosum* means, for Jung, an experience of the archetypal layers of the unconscious. The line between the psychological and the theological is drawn very fine, and Jung will sometimes seem inadvertently to cross over it when he explicates symbolic material in dreams, visions, and alchemical texts.

There is also the important element of secrecy in the connotations around the word *mysterium*. The Latin word is derived from the Greek *mystērion*, meaning secret rite or doctrine (known and practiced by certain initiated persons only), consisting of purifications, sacrificial offerings, processions, songs, etc. This is a reference to such famous ancient mystery cults as the Eleusinian Mysteries and the Mysteries of Isis, where the rites served as the means of initiation into the cult. Secrecy was seen as necessary for the effective transmission to the participants of the spiritual energies invoked in the rites and rituals. The "one who has been initiated" was called a *mystēs*. Initiation implies the transformation of identity that the initiates experience as they move from the status of applicant to graduate. Today we hear a faint echo of this practice in our induction and graduation ceremonies in schools and universities. We might call someone with a Master's degree a *mystés*, an initiated one.

Most interesting and closely associated with the importance of secrecy is that the word *mysterion* derives from the basic Greek word *myein* — "to close, to shut" — which perhaps refers to closing the lips in secrecy or to closing the eyes in preparation for the revelation that would take place as a result of the rites. At the base of etymologies, one often comes upon something very simple and, as we say, archetypal. In the Mysteries, we see that silence, secrecy, and being closed off from the world in a sacred space, typically in a structure resembling a cave that symbolized the womb, are emphasized.

From the title of Jung's book with that word, *Mysterium,* front and center, we clearly receive notice that what we are about to enter into here is a discussion of something secret, sacred, and touching on the archetypal powers of psychological and spiritual transformation.

Like the first part of the book's title, the second part, *Coniunctionis,* is of critical importance for understanding the work's meaning. In Latin, it means simply "bond" or "union." In chemistry, it would indicate the union of two elements to create a compound. Jung writes at the beginning of the first chapter of *Mysterium*: "The factors which come together in the coniunctio are conceived as opposites, either confronting one another in enmity or attracting one another in love."[28] And in a footnote, he quotes from a text by the alchemist Ripley: "The coniuntio is the uniting of separated qualities or an equalizing of principles."[29]

As a predecessor to chemistry, alchemy worked with materials that were considered basic, like the elements in modern chemistry. The four basic elements were air, fire, water, and earth. There were also the three chemical elements: salt, sulfur, and mercury. The materials for the experiments were collected according to secret recipes, and when placed together, the mixture was called *prima materia,*

---

[28] C.G. Jung, *Mysterium Coniunctionis*, para. 1.
[29] *Ibid.*, ftn. 1. From *Theatrum chemicum*, II, p. 128.

which was placed into a suitable container for processing, usually a vessel or flask. The Adept then applied some secret alchemical methods to the *massa confusa* in the vessel in order to sort the mixture into pairs of opposites. These pairs were meant to bond together and join another pair, forming a quaternity, out of which new compounds would be created.

The process would begin with raw materials and pass through a series of operations (*calcinatio*, *solutio*, *coagulatio*, *sublimatio*, *mortificatio*, *separatio*, *coniunctio*), and eventually, the result would be something new that could not be found in nature: a new creation. This process was seen as a transformation from the base assembled materials at the outset to the noble product at the conclusion, and it was seen as mysterious because the science was not available to understand the material basis of the process. Into this process, the alchemists projected a large variety of images and meanings. It was Jung's genius to apply psychological understanding to the projective processes and to understand the alchemical opus as symbolic of the individuation process.

As Jung interprets the alchemical imagination, the opposites that the alchemists sought to unite on a material level represented features of the psyche — anima, animus, shadow, etc. The union, or integration, of these is the goal of individuation in Jung's theory.

Since the entire opus depends on *coniunctio*, an important question would be: What can motivate the union of the opposites? The magical "transformation factor" in the unification process in alchemy was mercury, symbolized by the figure Mercurius. Mercury was the medium, or bath, in which the conjunction of opposites, as represented by sulfur (the masculine) and salt (the feminine), took place. As an androgynous figure combining the opposites in himself, Mercurius was the catalyst for the process. Without this uniting factor, the opposites would not be brought to the point of interacting with one another. In the alchemical lexicon, Mercurius was defined as the beginning and the end of the process, and indeed as the process itself. Because he was imaged as androgenous, the opposites are both represented in this figure, and this is why he is able to bring them together. He is like a model or template, a symbol of conjunction of the opposites.

Mercurius might be compared to the force of gravity in nature: He is able to pull the separated and oppositional elements toward himself and holds them in place. Mysteriously, too, he dissolves their antagonism, like a diplomat soothing the tempers of oppositional political parties and creating the conditions for dialogue. Without the force of gravity, the universe would simply disperse and disappear into empty space. In psychological terms, Mercurius represents the power of the self to hold the psychic pieces in place as they evolve, to bring them into relation to one another, and to secure their positions in a structure of wholeness. In Kabbalah, the power responsible for the structure of balance among the 10 Sefirot ("emanations" or "opposites") that are represented in the Kabbalistic Tree of Life is Ein Sof, the Infinite. Psychologically interpreted, Ein Sof is the self. Jung discusses Kabbalah and the Sefirot in Chapter 5 of *Mysterium*.

In psychology, the process of reconciliation among the various pairs of opposites — most notably animus and anima, and persona and shadow — is conceived as an extended process of integration whereby ego-consciousness is relieved of its attachment to one side of the opposition, and the unconscious is similarly released from its domination by the other. They can then become a structured totality under the auspices of the self, while still leaving room for the parts to remain discrete and not become melted together into a single homogeneous unit, a kind of "black hole," where gravity is so strong that even photons (light) cannot escape. The goal is to bring the opposites into a delicate and sustained relationship with one another, not to eliminate one in favor of the other. The Tree of Life, like the Rebis, symbolizes this: the two columns on the right and left of the Tree representing Judgment and Mercy, while the two heads of the Rebis figure represent animus and anima in one body.

Mercurius is a mysterious figure in alchemy, a magician. In one of Jung's most fascinating alchemical writings, "The Spirit Mercurius," he interprets Mercurius as "the spirit of the unconscious," which on behalf of the self directs the individuation process on its serpentine path toward the goal of psychological integration and wholeness. It was this mysterious, magnetic, magical "spirit" that Jung detected at work in the background of his own individuation process (as "the spirit of the depths" in *Liber Novus*), as well as in his patients' psychological material as it evolved in the analytic process.

In *Mysterium,* Jung writes of Mercurius that "he *is* this marriage on account of his androgynous form."[30] Like the Holy Spirit in Christian theology who binds the Trinitarian Godhead into a stable One-in-Three unity, Mercurius brings into a state of multifaceted unity the many "opposites" of the

---

[30] C.G. Jung, *Mysterium Coniunctionis*, para. 12.

self. It is the genius of Mercurius that the many do not disappear into a singularity but rather retain their unique qualities and facets, diamondlike, while joining the wholeness structure of the mandala. Thus, room for diversity is preserved while unity is attained.

This is the answer to the dilemma of "the One or the Many." It has often been discussed among Jungian authors: Is the personality multiple and many, or is it one? Polytheism or monotheism? The answer is: "both" — diversity in unity; unity in diversity. This is the only realistic and sustainable goal for individuation given the complexity of the human personality. And this is the net implication of the *Coniunctionis* in the title of the text: it is "unity," but it does not deny or eliminate diversity and differentiation.

The Conjunction

Unio Naturalis

The sixth and final chapter of *Mysterium Coniunctionis* offers some practical information about the stages of individuation that concern union rather than separation. Jung draws on the work of Gerhardt Dorn, arguably his favorite alchemical author, to describe three stages of coniunctio: 1) the achievement of *unio mentalis*, which consists of a union of soul and spirit; 2) the union of *unio mentalis* with the body, which has been left behind in the preceding stage; and 3) the union with *unus mundus*.

Dorn's model begins with an initial state in which soul and body are fused called *unio naturalis*, which speaks of a natural, instinctual life in the body.

A change is instigated at some point, and *unio naturalis* undergoes a process of separation (*separatio*) of soul from body. It is a kind of awakening. Consciousness takes stock of the situation and introduces a differentiation between the desires of the body and the thoughts of the soul. A period of liminality ensues in which soul moves to spirit and unites with it. A new type of consciousness and identity develops, which is no longer based on ego-body and ego-persona identifications. Thus, the first stage of Dorn's transformation model completes itself. He calls the result *unio mentalis*.

Unio Mentalis

According to Jung, *unio mentalis* describes a psychologically aware state of mind that is no longer dominated by somatic needs and instinctual drives or persona demands for social approval. A new type of individual freedom and inner direction is achieved at this stage of individuation. To reach this state of union of soul and spirit, the "body" has been left behind in a sort of suspended animation state. It continues to exist but in a deathlike sleep. In other words, what the body represents is no longer determinative of state of mind. The cognitive (*mentalis*) outweighs the somatic-emotional at this level of development.

Unio mentalis is then followed by a second stage of conjunction, which consists of a reunion with the body.

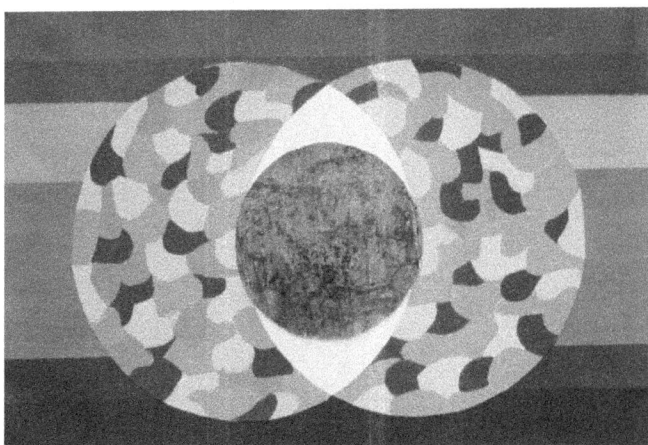

Unio Mentalis et Soma

What was left out as a determinative factor is now taken up, reanimated, and given a new mission. The body is no longer dominant with respect to the ego; rather, the ego and the body now stand in service of *unio mentalis*. What develops in

155

this stage is a practical, morally enlightened, engaged attitude toward life in this world. It is not otherworldly but rather grounded in the world of social and material existence. The body has been taken up into the more conscious state of *unio mentalis* and is now included in its purposes and activities.

Finally, there is a third *coniunctio* with what the medieval writers called the *unus mundus*.

Unus Mundus

Unus mundus means "the one world." The phrase refers to a commonly shared medieval perception that everything that exists belongs to and within a single, unified reality. It is the alpha and omega of existence: the origin and the underlying reality. In Jungian psychology, it would correspond to the collective unconscious whose center and circumference is the self. In scholastic philosophy, it was credited to the spirit of God. In other words, it is the Holy Spirit, i.e., the spirit of Love. To unite personal identity with this ultimate transcendent reality results in a spiritual life that is similarly all-embracing. In this final result of Dorn's three conjunctions, all of the opposites are united in a totality with both immanent (the body) and transcendent (the soul and spirit) dimensions.

The individual's ego-consciousness, moreover, is preserved within this matrix (or "field") of transpersonal wholeness, so diversity (i.e., individuality) and unity (i.e., totality) are both maintained. This is neither an individualistic nor a totalitarian model. It is a *mysterium coniunctionis* of pluralism and unity, the many and the one.

The three stages of individuation represent a progressive movement toward ever-greater consciousness. And it moves ego-consciousness toward a state of realization that inner and outer are deeply interconnected. The "whole" includes the individual and all that exists — local and world community, global environment, cosmos. This final development of consciousness presupposes, of course, the deep transformations that have been described in the previous chapters of *Mysterium*. There is no discount ticket to this goal of individuation.

This three-stage description of individuation is a process directed toward ultimate wholeness, and it offers a practical model for thinking about the development toward consciousness that can be observed in analysis. As the subject undergoes a sustained confrontation with the shadow and engages with the figures of the collective unconscious in active imagination, a sense of an inner world emerges that includes the ego but does not make it central. The ego is relativized as the Self comes into view and shows its centrality. Dante's experience as expressed in *Paradiso* is a beautifully stated religious version of this psychological vision. The final Canto of *The Divine Comedy* is a religious epiphany that results in his most profound transformation:

> already I could feel my being turned —
> instinct and intellect balanced equally
> as in a wheel whose motion nothing jars —
> by the Love that moves the Sun and the
> other stars.[31]

Conclusion

The distilled message of *Mysterium Coniunctionis* could be stated as a promise: Wholeness comes at a high price. But no matter how much you suffer for its sake, you will be rewarded. No suffering for the sake of wholeness will go unrewarded. The reward is manifold: knowledge of the inner world, personal and collective; a sense of the mystery of the Self in its personal and impersonal dimensions; the establishment of a stable sense of unity within diversity; a vision of purpose and meaning in life; the acquisition of perspective on self and other without judgment and yet with differentiated perception of positives and negatives included in the mandala of wholeness. One could add more features,

---

[31] Dante, *The Divine Comedy, Paradiso* XXXIII: 143-146.

but the general idea is that the personality that was divided, scattered and largely unconscious is made whole and is now far more conscious. The union is mysterious, necessarily so, yet tangible in the form of images of the self and a stable state of consciousness that embraces the opposites to the greatest extent possible.

This way does not offer perfection but rather wholeness. I think it can be concluded without the least qualification that this was Jung's ultimate objective in his own life and for those who read his works, engage in analysis, and seriously pursue individuation. *Mysterium Coniunctionis* — his last book — says it all.

"Individuation" and/vs. "Enlightenment"

The process of individuation as described by C.G. Jung and the spiritual practices of the East as depicted in texts such as *The Secret of the Golden Flower* of Chinese alchemy and *The Ten Ox-Herding Pictures* of Zen Buddhism share a common goal: the transformation of consciousness. By this is meant, as a start, the transformation from sheer brutish egoism and sensuality to a state of consciousness that transcends such basic (and normal) human desires and attains to a broader view of life's meaning. At a more advanced and deeper level, transformation of consciousness pertains to overcoming the habitual patterns of thought that become locked into place by routine and repetition, the conditioning of the prevailing collective culture, and the defensive psychological formations created by traumatic life experiences. Both Jung's understanding of the individuation process and the spiritual practices of the East have the objective of transforming consciousness along these basic lines as the goal of development. Certainly, there are differences in practice and in the terms that are used to describe how the process of transformation unfolds, but the objective is similar (if not identical). It is the purpose of this paper to accentuate the similarities over the differences while keeping in mind the very dissimilar cultural contexts from which they originate. In my view, they are converging increasingly as a global culture gradually takes form. The outcomes of

161

advanced Jungian psychoanalysis more and more resemble the advanced psychological attainments of Eastern spiritual practices, and vice versa.

Since the beginning of the 19th century in the West, and with increasing depth and intensity in the late 20th century and into the 21st century, considerable interest has been directed toward the spiritual practices and disciplines of the East and in drawing comparisons between East and West with regard to possibilities for advanced psychological and spiritual development. Many people have read the translated spiritual classics of the East, and many have learned the practices of yoga and meditation. Jung himself was heavily engaged in this study, and while he frequently cited major differences, he also looked for similarities based on archetypal factors in the psyche. In fact, it was these similarities between individuation as he experienced it in himself and with his patients and what he discovered in the Chinese alchemical text *The Secret of the Golden Flower* sent to him in German translation by his friend Richard Wilhelm that led him to conclude that there is an archetypal basis for the individuation process. "I devoured the manuscript at once," he writes, "for the text gave me undreamed-of confirmation of my ideas about the mandala and the circumambulation of the center. That was the first event which broke through my isolation. I became aware of an affinity; I could establish ties with something and someone."[1] From his brilliant commentary on the Chinese text, we receive the strong message that there are important and essential underlying similarities between ancient Chinese spiritual practices and the individuation process.

---

[1] C.G. Jung, *Memories Dreams, Reflections*, p. 197.

A question to be considered, however, is this: Individuation presupposes the singularity and uniqueness of every human being (individuals) and promotes each person's self-realization as the goal of psychological development. Is this not the exact contrary and opposite of the Eastern project of reaching enlightenment (Chinese "wu" and Japanese "satori"), which aims at destroying uniqueness and individuality (ego) in favor of "the unity of all" or "Buddha nature" and awareness of "the void"? How can these two projects be reconciled? Or can't they? The West's emphasis on the separate and individual ego, the East's emphasis on nonego and unity — are they irreconcilable? I believe they are not, and that is because of Jung's understanding of individuation as it unfolds in its most advanced stages. Jung's account makes it possible to narrow, if not completely close, the gap between Enlightenment as realized by people who practice the methods of the spiritual traditions of the East and individuation as realized by people who pursue the path of psychological development using the methods of Jungian psychology.

To make this argument, I advert to three advanced stages in the individuation process described by Jung in his late work, *Mysterium Coniunctionis*. There, Jung turns to the alchemical transformations described by Gerhard Dorn, the 16th-century physician, philosopher, and alchemist, which can be summarized as follows:

1) The attainment through mental discipline to self-knowledge, which is named *unio mentalis* in the writings of Dorn.

2) The embodiment of this attained state of transformed consciousness in the form of action in the world.

3) The connection of the individual consciousness to *unus mundus*, thus producing a nondualistic awareness of the interconnectedness of all existent being.

Jung's discussion of these three stages of individuation is found in the last chapter of *Mysterium*, "The Conjunction." Each of these stages has significant resonance with stages on the way to Enlightenment as depicted in *The Ten Ox-Herding Pictures* of Chan/Zen Buddhism.

Stage One — From *Unio Naturalis* to the Achievement of *Unio Mentalis*

The first task in tackling the challenge of individuation is to achieve a state of unified consciousness. Following Dorn, Jung calls this "*unio mentalis*" (Latin: "union of mind"). This is not a simple matter, as we shall see, and it has many levels.

Psychological life begins in the form of a kind of archipelago, a scattering of somewhat solid landmasses of consciousness in a sea of psychic fluidity. Out of these bits of consciousness there eventually emerges a dominant entity, which we call the ego, a center of consciousness that responds to a name, and the other bits establish more or less stable links to it and become associated as attached memories and fantasies. This is the earliest attempt at *unio mentalis*. In the course of childhood and adolescence, this "I" achieves a more extensive identity through a process of projection and introjection, a development that Michael Fordham discusses as deintegration and integration cycles.[2] The identity that is formed and developed in this early phase is made up of bits of

---

[2] M. Fordham, *Explorations into the Self,* Pt. I: 3.

family and ancestral material, cultural patterns and influences, and inherent pieces of the self (the intrapsychic contribution). This unity is fragile, however, and given to falling apart (dissociating) under stress and pressure, regressing to earlier states of identity in childhood, and coming under the massive influence of emotions generated by unconscious complexes that are often created by split-off and repressed traumas. It is also largely embedded in and associated with the body, an identity between mind and body. While young persons may feel themselves as individuals, actually they are not such to any significant extent. This young and not yet mature ego-identity is more or less a typical representative of a collective pattern established in the prevalent culture of family, peer groups, and society. It is a state that Dorn called *unio naturalis*, a natural union of psyche and body.

Individuation in the sense that Jung speaks of it — as the attainment of uniqueness, self-knowledge, and full realization of inner potentials — cannot begin effectively until a severe reduction has taken place in this first unity, that is, until this conglomerate of amassed bits and pieces of psychic material has been taken apart and the center of awareness, the innermost kernel of ego-consciousness, has been freed from extraneous contaminations. This process of analysis and separation is the forerunner and presupposition for achieving *unio mentalis* in the next phase. In *The Principle of Individuation*, I discuss this as the "separation movement" within the overall individuation process. The other great movement of individuation is "integration," which as we shall see takes place after separation is underway or completed and *unio mentalis* has come within reach.

The method for achieving this stage of *unio mentalis* in analytical psychology is the analysis of complexes, projections, defenses, and dreams. The purpose of this is to clear away whatever stands in the way of gaining access to purified consciousness, that is, to gain a state of ego-consciousness that is not distorted by complexes, projections, wishes, fears, cultural biases, and cultural conditioning. In short, as Jung writes: "... the ego-personality's coming to terms with its own background, the shadow, corresponds to the union of spirit and soul in *the unio mentalis* ..."[3] This is slow work and often takes quite a long time to achieve. It is similar to what meditation seeks to achieve in Ch'an Buddhism, for instance. There is a passage in "Master Hsu Yun's Discourses and Dharma Words," which Jung was reading in his last days (the book *Ch'an and Zen Teaching: First Series* was found on his bedside table when he died), that reads as follows:

> "... when the sun rises and sunlight enters (the house) through an opening, the dust is seen moving in the ray of light whereas the empty space is unmoving. Therefore, that which is still is voidness and that which moves is dust." Foreign dust illustrates false thinking and voidness illustrates self-nature. ... This serves to illustrate the eternal (unmoving) self-nature which does not follow false thinking in its sudden rise and fall.[4]

---

[3] C.G. Jung, *Mysterium Coniunctionis*, *CW* 14, para. 707.
[4] C. Luk (ed. and transl.), *Ch'an and Zen Teaching*, p. 36.

In a similar vein, about *unio mentalis* Jung writes: "The declared aim of the treatment is to set up a rational, spiritual psychic position over against the turbulence of the emotions."[5] In the alchemical metaphor, this involves separating the soul (symbolized by water) from the body (symbolized by solid matter) and uniting it with the spirit (symbolized by air). This is achieved by boiling the water off the *prima materia* in the flask, allowing the moisture to rise as steam and condensing at the top, the droplets, representing the union of soul and spirit.

In the Zen Buddhist picture series *The Ten Ox-Herding Pictures*, this stage of consciousness is initially represented in Picture 6, "Riding the Ox Home."[6]

---

[5] Jung, *Mysterium Coniunctionis*, para. 696.
[6] Pictures from https://upload.wikimedia.org/wikipedia/commons/3/3f/Oxherding_pictures%2C_No._6.jpg

This picture, which is the culmination of the search for and retrieval and taming of the Ox in Pictures 1-5, symbolizes a state of harmony between conscious and unconscious and sets the stage for the developments depicted in Pictures 7-10.

In Zen Buddhism, the Ox symbolizes much more than only the realm of instincts, as we might mistakenly interpret it. It is also a symbol of the "self-nature," to use the term from Master Hsu Yun's *Discourses*. To find it and bring it into relation with consciousness is a tremendous achievement, but it is not yet *unio mentalis* in the complete sense.

Similarly, in Jung's understanding of the unconscious, the shadow is the doorway to deeper layers that ultimately include the transcendent self. The achievement of *unio mentalis* is more than attainment of rational control over the emotions. It is self-knowledge in a deep sense of the word: "The *unio mentalis* … means knowledge of oneself … the alchemists regarded the self as a substance incommensurable with the ego, hidden in the body, and identical with the image of God. … The psychic preparation [of *unio mentalis*] is therefore an attempt … to bring about a union of opposites in accordance with the great Eastern philosophies, and to establish for this purpose a principle freed from the opposites and similar to the *atman* or *tao* … today we would describe [this] as a transcendental principle. This 'unum' is *nirdvandva* (free from the opposites), like the *atman* (self)."[7] Here we see Jung explicitly bringing the individuation process into contact with Eastern religion and philosophy.

Jung's *Liber Novus* is a story of investigation and disidentification from archetypal fantasies, a further step in

---

[7] *Ibid.*, para. 711.

the attainment of *unio mentalis*. In Pictures 7, 8, and 9 of the *Ox-Herding* Series, we see clearly depicted the process of cleansing the "doors of perception" and arriving at a state of deep self-knowledge of the type Jung describes in his discussion of *unio mentalis*. Picture 7 shows the man gazing serenely at the landscape with a mountain and the moon on the horizon.

His consciousness is undisturbed by complexes or projections. He is simply "seeing." Picture 8 shows the Enzo, symbol of the Void, or the experience of pure "self-nature," as Master Hsu Yun calls it.

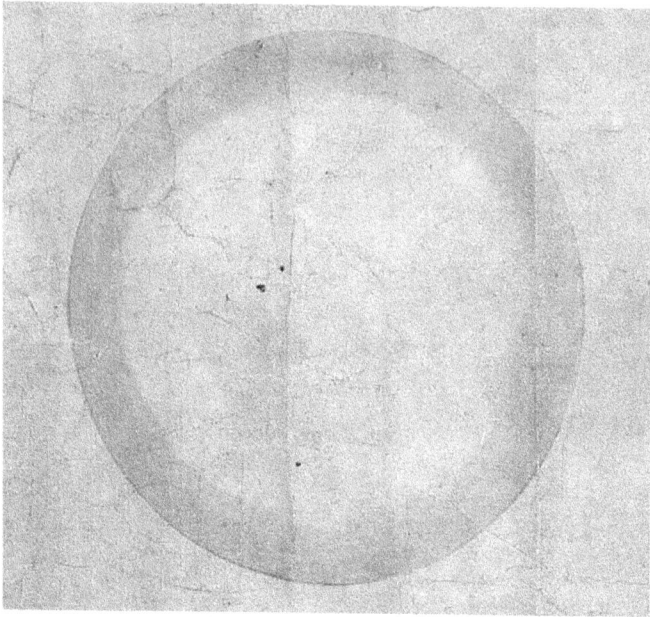

This is a breakthrough, out of ego into Self-awareness. Jung would depict this in his mandala paintings in *Liber Novus*. There is no "person" in the picture, only the mandala, which is a symbol of wholeness. The text for this picture reads:

> Whip, rope, ox and man alike belong to Emptiness.
> So vast and infinite the azure sky
> that no concept of any sort can reach it.
> Over a blazing fire a snowflake cannot survive.
> When this state of mind is realized
> comes at last comprehension
> of the spirit of the ancient patriarchs.

And in Picture 9, "Returning to the Source," we see the roots of an old tree exposed to consciousness.

This picture shows a state of consciousness of archetypal sources beyond personal history of ego development: "the spirit of the ancient patriarchs." Even the deepest roots of the psyche are exposed to the awareness of consciousness. It is equivalent to supreme enlightenment. This is the goal of the analytic process as well, which is dedicated to gaining self-knowledge through separation from all identifications and entanglements with unconscious contents. While this is a goal seldom reached, it is always kept in mind as the ultimate attainment of *unio mentalis*.

Stage 2 — Uniting *Unio Mentalis* with the Body

As we see in the *Ox-Herding Pictures*, the "body" of the individual person disappears in this ascent to *unio mentalis*. In other words, one leaves the everyday world (*Samsara*) for a time. Now the challenge is to come back to the "body" in a different way and not to "fall back" into the old traps and habits. The awareness achieved in Pictures 6-9 must somehow enter into practical reality and make a difference in attitude and behavior. This return is depicted in the *Ox-Herding Picture* 10, "Entering the Market."

In Jungian psychoanalysis, we look for change not only in a removed consciousness but also in attitude and behavior. The term "transformation" covers both the "aesthetic" and the "ethical" dimensions of life. One can enjoy and appreciate the journey to greater consciousness by writing and drawing and painting one's dreams, active imaginations, and other inner visionary experiences, but this process of individuation must also make a difference in everyday life. Picture 10 of the *Ox-Herding Series* is titled "entering the marketplace." The verses for this picture are:

> Bare-chested, bare-footed, he comes into the marketplace.
> Muddied and dust-covered, how broadly he grins!
> Without recourse to mystic powers, Withered trees he swiftly brings to bloom.

What this movement toward transformation of attitude and behavior aims for is the penetration of the consciousness achieved in *unio mentalis* into what Jung calls in his *Liber Novus,* "the spirit of the times." We live in a world that is deeply conditioned by history and cultural complexes. The aim of the work toward achieving *unio mentalis* is to separate from this; the aim of the work of integrating the "body" into *unio mentalis* is to bring this consciousness into the world where it will make a difference in everyday life ("the marketplace"). Because the shadow has been made conscious in *unio mentalis*, the actions taken in this stage are relatively free of its malicious side-effects.

Stage 3 — *Unus Mundus* — The Union of Personal with Impersonal Self

Of this stage Jung writes: "The thought Dorn expresses by the third stage of conjunction is universal: It is the relation or identity of the personal with the suprapersonal atman, and of the individual *tao* with the universal *tao*."[8] In this passage, Jung again brings together West and East, drawing on the 16th-century European philosopher and alchemist Gerhard Dorn and Chinese Daoism. Jung finds a point of unity in their visions of spiritual and psychological development, and he goes on to relate this to the individuation process. Here we arrive at the highest degree of conjunction: "the union of the whole man with the unus mundus ... a union with the world — not the world of multiplicity as we see it but with a potential world, the eternal Ground of all empirical being, just as the self is the ground and origin of the individual personality past, present and future."[9]

The final picture in the *Ox-Herding* series implies this stage of individuation. The text reads: "Withered trees he swiftly brings to bloom." This means that he is so deeply connected to *unus mundus* that without doing anything, his mere presence is salutary. Synchronicity accompanies him as he walks through the marketplace. His teaching is not by words alone, although he does speak and teach, but the influence of his presence extends beyond the range of his personality and touches the surrounding world through the channel of mystical unity with the *unus mundus*. This is a stage of individuation in which conscious and unconscious

---

[8] C.G. Jung, *Mysterium Coniunctionis*, para. 762.
[9] *Ibid.*, para. 760.

are unified, not only the personal unconscious but the collective unconscious as well. This takes Stage 2 with its strong ethical accent a step further to include the ecological dimension in the broadest sense of the word — nature itself. Stage 3 brings consciousness of "the empathy of all things" in a wide context, both of space and time.

Conclusion

I hope I have made my argument that there are significant points of connection and similarity between the Western psychological concept of individuation in its advanced stages and the Eastern vision of Enlightenment in some of its more visible aspects. These can be seen by comparing Jung's late theory of stages of individuation with *The Ten Ox-Herding Pictures* of Zen Buddhism and various Ch'an teachings. On a purely cultural level, the paths seem very different because of cultural forms like intense and focused meditation over a long period of time on the one hand and the work of Jungian psychoanalysis with its more intermittent regularity and emphasis on dreams and active imagination on the other. On a more subtle and profound level, however, there appear to be important similarities. This means that ancient Eastern wisdom and modern Western psychological and spiritual development can walk comfortably side by side, reaching out to each other and learning from one other. Their points of reference may be different, but their respective experiences of transcendence and the transformation of consciousness and attitude are, if not identical, very close to one another. Both know of synchronicity, *unus mundus*, *unio mentalis* and corresponding ethical action.

What Jung has contributed to the Western understanding of psychological development is the introverted
aspect, the "self-liberating power of the introverted mind,"
as he says in his "Commentary on *The Tibetan Book of the
Great Liberation.*"[10] Thus, he brings individuation into close
relation to Eastern practices of meditation and the achievement of "one mind" and enlightenment. In both, duality is
resolved in favor of a unified world with subjective and
objective divisions and splits healed and overcome in what
Erich Neumann, Jung's most brilliant student, terms "the
dissolution of the self's form and ... the actualization of the
anonymous self-field."[11] Neumann references Zen and speaks
of the masters who, "in their acts and in their being, and in
the unity of inner and outer, ego and self,"[12] demonstrate this
degree of individuation.

---

[10] C.G. Jung, "Psychological Commentary on 'The Tibetan Book of the Great
Liberation,'" para. 773.
[11] E. Neumann, "The Psyche and the Reality Planes," p. 61.
[12] *Ibid.*

The Mystery of Creativity —
A Journey in Pictures

In the previous chapter, I attempted to draw a parallel between the Eastern goal of Enlightenment as expressed in *The Ten Ox-Herding Pictures* of Zen Buddhism and the Western vision of psychological and spiritual development as outlined in the Jungian account of the individuation process. This chapter is a commentary on a series of 10 paintings made by Diane Stanley, a contemporary artist, in response to studying and meditating upon the *Ox-Herding Picture* series. In these images, she captures the journey as process that leads to the mystery of creativity. The pictures, which the artist herself titled, depict a process that is at once ancient and postmodern.

I will consider the images that emerged from her meditations as a depiction of an archetypal psychological process in the service of individuation in the second half of life. They represent a development that begins in uncertainty and confusion and culminates in a brilliant release of creativity from out of the Self. The pattern of this psychological journey is archetypal, timeless, and universal. In the Zen series, this is regarded as a journey to Enlightenment; in the present series, it is shown as a journey to the Self and Creativity. The basic pattern of the journeys is the same, while the outcome appears to be different. In Zen, the net result is joyful tranquility-in-living; in this series, it is exuberant creativity-in-the-present. The difference between the two outcomes may be less than it seems at first impression.

....

Picture 1: *Something is Missing*

The artist's title for the first picture in the series shows the starting point for the journey that follows. The subject discovers that something is missing. This comes as a sudden realization — consciousness dawns and takes notes of the lack of something essential. What is this "something"?

I will take "the missing" to be "soul" and assume that this is similar to the condition Jung writes about at the beginning of *The Red Book: Liber Novus* when he calls out plaintively: "My Soul, where are you? Do you hear me?"[1] The soul has vanished, and in this first image of the series, we see this feeling of emptiness represented by the hole in the center of the picture.

The experience of loss of soul typically happens at midlife, but it can happen most anytime, especially for

---

[1] C.G. Jung, *The Red Book: Liber Novus*. Reader's Edition, p. 127.

creative personalities, when disillusionment sets in and there is no energy for living in the old patterns and routines. How one has lived before no longer works. It has lost its meaning. This state of mind can come about in many ways. It may be something like burnout, which is a regrettably common condition among professional and working people today. Psychotherapists often confront this in their patients. People arrive at a dead end, whether in their relational life or in their occupational and professional life, and they don't have any more zest for it. No "flow" to lift them and give them a sense of meaningful activity. Or they go through a bitter divorce or lose a parent or a child. "The yeast was out of the bread of the land," as Karen Blixen wrote so poignantly in *Out of Africa* of the loss of her friend, Berkeley Cole. People may continue to go through the motions, but they do so without hope or love.

When the soul goes missing in life, the guiding vision and the energy and meaning that have sustained it vanish. This moment of realization can be devastating, but it can also mark an important first step in the process of further individuation. The shocking realization that what had been constructed previously was based on projections and faulty assumptions leads to a collapse of the structure. The future is impossible to imagine. But this is the beginning of a journey into the unknown, as it was for Dante when his way forward was blocked and he found himself alone one day in a dark wood. And this was the realization that brought Jung, too, to cry out, "My soul, where are you?" at the beginning of his journey inward. The first picture in the present series draws us into the same condition.

179

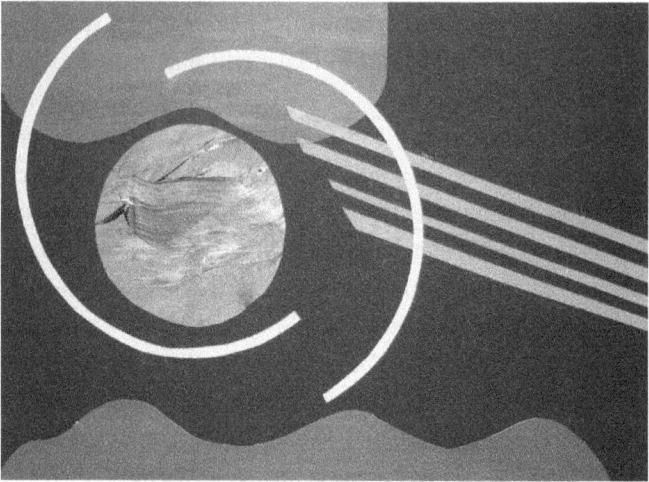

Picture 2: *A Glimpse of Insight*

Picture 2 signals a shift in mood. The four strong lines coming from the right, the side of consciousness, perceive a full, round object in the darkness of the unconscious on the left. It's a discovery! The picture shows a considerable surge of energy. What does this glimpse of insight reveal? How does this come to a person?

Suppose you are in that state of confusion and disorientation and stumbling through life without a clear sense of direction, and a book unexpectedly falls into your hands. You open it and start reading, and suddenly you find yourself thinking, "Well, this is something interesting. I never thought of this before." Maybe it's a book of philosophy or psychology. Maybe it's Jung's autobiography — that was my experience. Or it's a lecture. You suddenly get a glimpse of that "something" out there in the opaque darkness. "Dreams!

Look at your dreams" is the message of *Memories, Dreams, Reflections*. And now you have a clue, and you can choose to pursue it. There is a glimmer of hope that a way may be found. The insight resonates. And it's enough to inspire you to search in a particular direction, to try to get closer to that newly discovered object in the dark.

For some people, this insight actually comes in a numinous dream that sets them in a new direction. It could also come as a projection of fascination upon someone who seems to offer inspiration, in whom you see wisdom or something magical like genius. People who met Goethe, for instance, and engaged him in conversation, which was not easy, often went away in amazement. Such a meeting occurred with the 30-year-old Marianna Jung, which transformed her briefly from an actress and dancer into a world-class poet for her contributions to Goethe's famous *West-östlicher Divan*. The charisma catches your attention, and you decide to pursue it. It's the beginning of recovering the sense of soul that has gone lost.

Picture 3: *The Work is Difficult & Dangerous*

In this picture, we see the struggle that ensues after the insight is grasped and its implications become evident. The insight leads to a profound recognition of the psyche's complexity. The inner world that opens up is fraught with conflicting tendencies. To regain soul and bring it back into a living relation with consciousness involves engaging seriously with the unconscious. This is the work of dealing with and suffering the opposites that are inherent in the Self and that energize the individuation process if they can be brought into relation with one another and harnessed for productive activity. In this painting, a large circle contains and draws to itself all the tendencies of the psyche — instinctual, psychological, social, political, and spiritual. As we see, they are jostling around and slamming against one another. It is not a harmonious scene. This is not paradise. Jung quotes the alchemist philosopher Hippolytus to describe the Self in this state:

> This Man is a single Monad, uncom-
> pounded and indivisible, yet compound-
> ed and divisible; love and at peace with
> all things yet warring with all things
> and at war with itself in all things' un-
> like and like itself, as it were a musical
> harmony containing all things. That
> single, undivided jot is the many-faced,
> thousand-eyed, and thousand-named jot
> of the iota. This is the emblem of that
> perfect and invisible Man.[2]

If one is to come into a conscious relationship with this paradoxical Self, it requires hard work to manage the sharp divisions. Shadow fights with persona, anima fights with animus, thinking fights with feeling, head with heart, good with bad, etc., etc. This is what Jung called "confrontation with the unconscious" in his autobiography, in which ego-consciousness is vigorously engaged with the paradoxical wholeness of the Self. The ego wants to simplify and run along on the old tracks, and the Self says, "No!" It's a battle for supremacy.

The issue is: You have an old life that is worn out, you have outgrown it, you have become disillusioned with it. The insight offers a new possibility for individuation and wholeness, but this creates a challenging tension. Partly, you want to cling to the old — the conservative part, the afraid part, the part that wants to hold onto prior certainties. There

---

[2] C.G. Jung, *Mysterium Coniunctionis*, para. 38.

is another part that rejects the old and says, "Come on! Let's take a risk and explore this new way." There is an inner conflict between the old attitude of ego-consciousness and the newly emergent Self that is now coming into play.

This happens to individuals, and it happens to collectives. Cultures are also called upon to shed their old skin from time to time and enter into a period of transformation to something new. It's a death and rebirth process. All of humanity stands precisely in this position today. Humans as a whole must change their attitude toward nature and the planet, and this provokes sharp and sometimes violent conflict between those who wish desperately to cling to past social, national, and cultural identities and what the newly emerging paradigm is moving toward and demanding. A global community is emerging, and this provokes conflict and confusion. Going on in the old way is blocked, the new is emerging, but it is not yet clear how the new attitude will ever come into being or what it will be.

Dante suffered this struggle at midlife when he found himself exiled from Florence and without the capacity to go forward with his previous interests and commitments. He was totally disillusioned with the vicious politics of his city, and he had to transform his sense of identity in a new and hostile environment. He was no longer the figure he had become in the old context. Now he awoke and found himself in a dark wood, his way forward blocked. To his surprise, a guide appears in the darkness, the poet Virgil, sent by the divine anima, Beatrice, to accompany him on his journey into and through the realms of the unconscious (Hell, Purgatory, Heaven). The work is difficult, but assistance is provided by the Self.

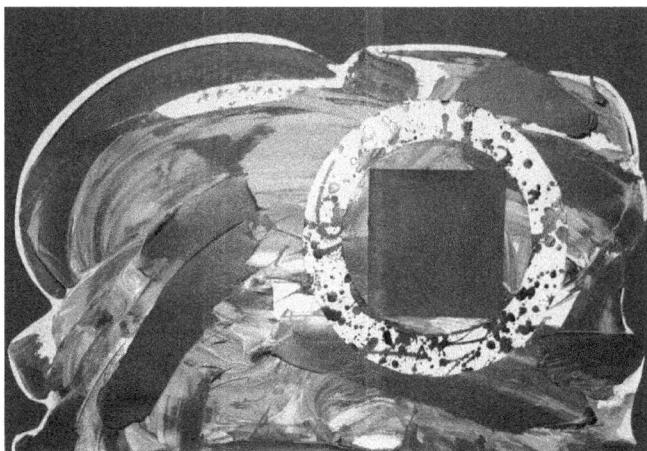

Picture 4: *Initiation into the Underworld*

We arrive in this picture in the shadow world of the unconscious. In analysis, this is a stage that Jung called "confession." It involves a deep dive into the shadowland of the psyche. Analysands look more deeply into their past and become acutely aware of the mistakes they have made, the wrong choices, the poor judgments that wounded themselves and others. It is the territory of shame and guilt. That's the darkness in this picture. A solid black square occupies the middle of it. One discovers, often for the first time, the shadow side of life that hasn't been taken into account before in a serious way. Most people just turn away from the shadow. If they catch a mere glimpse of it, or if somebody says something to them about their shadowy motives, their selfishness, greed, or envy, they deny it and project it onto the other person. "They don't know what they are talking about. They're projecting." But here the subject is facing it squarely.

Picture 5: *Meditatio*: *Dialogue*

This is a severe challenge to the ego and its capacity to suffer the indignities of facing the shadow, to actually endure and go through this darkness until it begins to change into the next stage, where dialogue can begin taking the place of conflict.

An important goal in Jungian psychoanalysis is to create the conditions for dialogue between ego and various parts of the Self. *Meditatio* is an inner dialogue, and it's a two-way exchange between ego-consciousness and the unconscious. A dialogue requires one to listen carefully and to respond to the other from an established position. In this picture, we see two semicircles meeting each other in the middle and almost touching. There are arrows coming toward a point of possible meeting. The two spheres are at the point of making contact with one another. Neither side is excessively dominant. They are reaching out to one another.

This type of inner dialogue takes place in *active imagination*. You are awake and present in the imaginary scene, and the imaginary figures appear and speak as well. This is the basis of the dialogue. Sometimes the inner figures say things you don't want to hear, and sometimes they speak of things you have never thought about and or ever considered. This type of exchange is needed to prepare for the change that is coming. The pictures in this Series depict a process of change, and this takes time and preparation. There are some sudden realizations and moments of insight along the way, but making the change real is a long and arduous process. In this picture, a dialogue has begun after the confrontation with the shadow in the previous picture. The two sides are now engaged with one another.

As a result of this dialogue between ego and the shadow within, the shadow of other people in one's surroundings also becomes more apparent. There's a moment when people in analysis will often come into a session and say something like: "I was at a party last night and I saw things I have never seen before. I saw what was going on underneath the surface, how people were jockeying with each other for position, how they were trying to put other people down, how they were mean, how they were selfish. I could see all of that in the room, although none of it was explicit." One's eyes are opened to shadow awareness.

It's an important realization that nobody is without shadow: no individual, no group or tribe, no nation. This must be faced and confronted before any change can take place and before a more profound dialogue with another can begin. In the dialogue, shadow reflections come into the foreground. The other can reflect, as in a mirror, your shadow back to you in ways that you can't see yourself. You have to be open to it and ready to receive it. The dialogue is an honest and open exchange, whether interpersonal or intrapsychic, between what

187

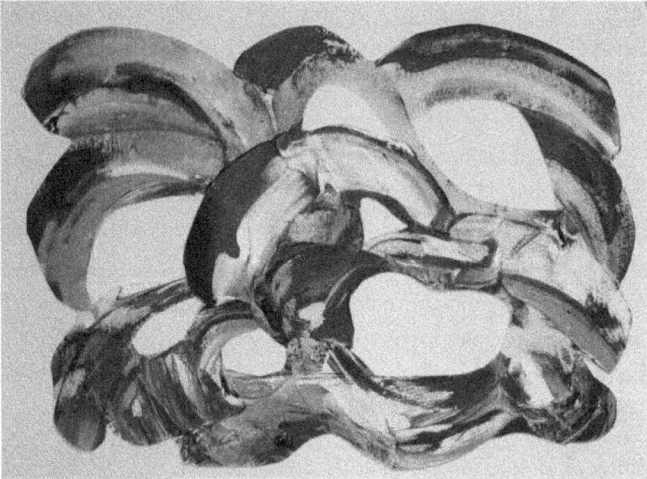

Picture 6: *Harmony & Movement in Relationship*

is conscious and what has been unconscious and projected, or just has never come out into the open before. This is a process that results later in transformation of consciousness.

In the sixth picture, we see a *mysterium coniunctionis*, as Jung wrote about it in his last book: the union and intermingling of the opposites that were previously in dialogue. There has been a big shift in the relationship between consciousness and the unconscious, and now true integration is possible as is the birth of the new attitude. It is a joyful moment of union in the process of individuation.

In the picture, there is no sign of conflict between right and left. There's a fluid, harmonious movement, a flowing together of mutually supportive energies, and one feels in tune with one's instincts and intuitions. This moment is depicted in Dante's *The Divine Comedy* toward the end of his journey through Purgatory when Virgil takes his leave of

188

Dante because he has reached the limit of his capacity as a guide and Dante has been purified in the fire. He gives Dante his blessing with these moving words:

"Expect no more of me in word or deed
here your will is upright, free, and whole."[3]

Virgil is saying that Dante can trust his own thoughts and his own intuitions. He doesn't need his guidance anymore. When people arrive at this stage, they can trust themselves. Think how far they have come from the first picture. Here, they can rely on their intuitions and impulses because they know them well and can use them as a guide. They can use their fantasies; their unconscious has become available to them. So, we see that wonderful flow in this picture between the right and the left moving in harmony and with both sides participating fully.

That brings us to the end of the first set in the series, which are preparation for what is now to come. The remaining pictures are the fulfillment of this preparation.

We come now to the initial image of the fulfillment of the process in the previous six pictures. This is a moment of clarity. The vision is stable and solid. There is no struggle, only a balanced state of mind. Here you see two halves of a sphere. One half is dark, the unconscious side on the left. The white lines coming in from the far left show a movement toward consciousness, pushing toward the right. The globe from Picture 2 has reappeared, a symbol of the Self hanging in the heavens like a full moon. On the right, we see a very well-put-together ego-consciousness. The right side and the left — conscious and unconscious — are related to each other

---

[3] Dante, *Purgatorio*, XXVII: 139-143.

Picture 7: *Coming to Rest*

and form a whole, like the Taoist yin-yang symbol. It's a very peaceful picture. After the struggles of preparation, now there is a waiting period, quiet and meditative.

This silent waiting period is important for what is to come. After the preparation, fulfillment doesn't suddenly happen. There is a pause, a period of resting, a transition, a period of waiting for the next stage to emerge. It is a time for patience. This might go on for a period of time, but there is psychic stability now. The subjects have come a long distance, have struggled mightily, and now can rely on a firm base within. They will know when the time will be right. They can trust the psyche. They can comfortably wait until the next movement comes that will lead them onward to the final and culminating fulfillment of the series.

There comes a sudden, dramatic change in the series. This picture features an illuminated circle against a black

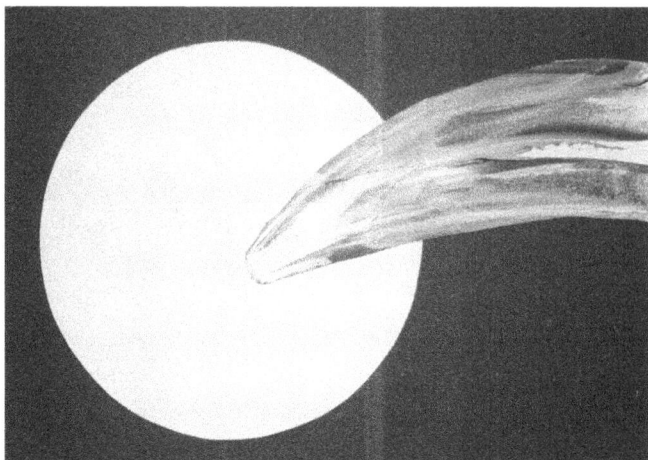

Picture 8: *Sudden Illumination*

background and a burst of energy either being radiated from or received by it. After a period of quiet meditation, everything changes in a brilliant flash of illumination. The transition period has transformed into an entirely new moment of consciousness. What is this?

This picture represents the climax of the process to this point. It also sets the stage for what is to come in the remainder of the series. It may be read as an annunciation: a signal of the future birth of the Self. The spirit (animus) and soul (anima), working in tandem, will become incarnated. In the *Ox-Herding Pictures*, this eighth position is occupied by the famous "Enzo," the empty circle. It is the apex of that series and represents a mystical experience of fullness-emptiness, the "Void." In the present series, the eighth picture has a strong dynamic element and is moving forward. It

191

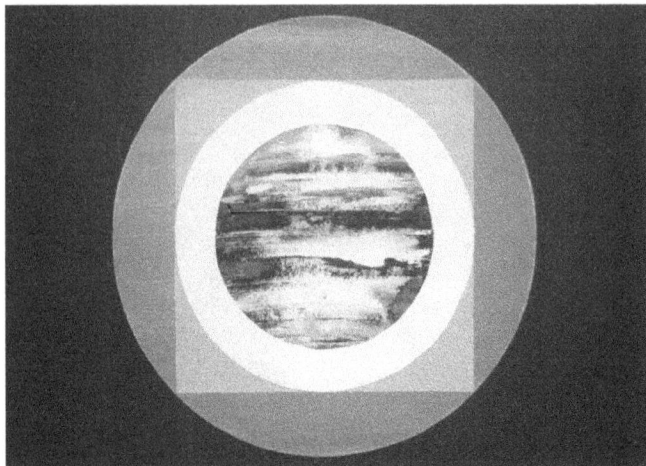

Picture 9: *The Source*

suggests futurity, the birth of a child. It is not an end state but the beginning of something new.

In Picture 9 the well-protected womb that houses the future incarnation of the Self is full. This is an incubation phase in the process. In the center are cloudlike formations; something is germinating there. It's a perfectly centered picture and represents the archetypal starting place of all that is. The dark frame around the outer circle is the deep cosmic unconsciousness out of which Being emerges as a mystery. The squaring of the circle and the encirclement of the square are representations of the idea of the paradox of wholeness. It's a picture of great psychological stability, and as a mandala, it's a symbol of the Self. This picture in the *Ox-Herding* series is titled "Reaching the Source" and shows a scene without Ox or a human figure, simply a scene of nature as Being itself. It is quietly impersonal.

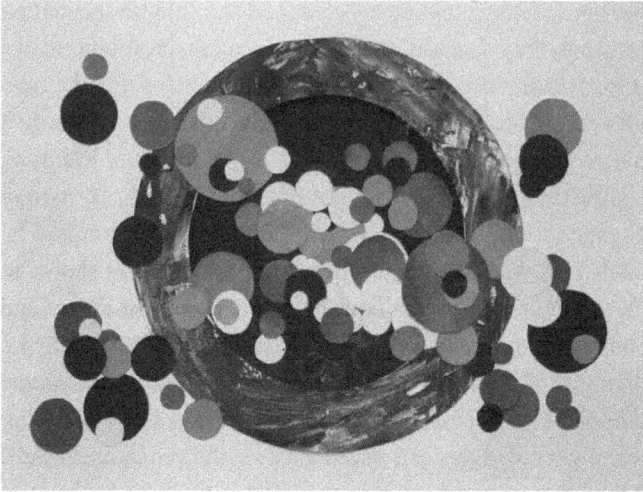

Picture 10: *The Creative*

Picture 10 represents an exuberant outburst of creativity from out of the darkness of the Self. Myriad bubbles are spilling out of the well-structured archetypal womb, the Self as womb of the world. Each circle can in time become a similar womb and give birth to new generations.

This moment is the culmination of a long period of preparation that featured a search and a struggle followed by fertilization and incubation. In our experience, this may go on for months or for years. In analysis, we witness this process extending over long periods of time. The results of this process are often remarkable.

I think of the biographies of people like Dante and Goethe and Jung and many others, whose greatest creative work was done following the loss of soul at earlier periods in their lives, after journeys through the archetypal world of the unconscious, and after prolonged and intense incubation of what they learned there. Jung's most profound works were written after the age of 60 and extended for the next 20 years. Like Goethe, who was in his 80s when he finished his greatest work, *Faust*, the epic story of his inner life, Jung completed and published his last and greatest book, *Mysterium Coniunctionis*, at the age of 80, only a few years before he died. This work came out of the kind of a process shown in these pictures: a process that begins in disillusionment and confusion, moves to insight and conflict, drops down into the darkness of the inner world and enters into dialogue with the others within, begins sorting things out and slowly moving toward recognition and acceptance of the paradoxical Self. All of that is in preparation for what is to come in the final movement to fulfillment.

What will eventually emerge from the last image, "The Creative," cannot be known in advance. It's full of potential, very complex, and shows a lot of possibilities. It's like a dandelion throwing its seeds into a meadow, all of them to flourish in the next spring. It's the beginning of what will come in the rest of life. This experience will form the basis for what this person will be able to contribute to culture. This type of creativity bursts out of the shell of the individual into the collective. The contributions that people make in their later years aren't specifically for their own well-being or their career advancement and personal goals. They are gifts to culture and to the evolution of consciousness in culture at large. Creations that come out of the kind of developmental process depicted in the pictures of the series have a tremendous impact on future generations and help them to orient themselves to the truth.

The fact is, we all have to go through this process if we are going to be creative in the second half of life. We can't merely rely on studying the creativity of those who have gone before us. We also have to suffer the process. Only then can we get to the stage of fulfillment forecast at the end of the series. The paintings depict this transformational process in a unique, artistic, and deeply felt communication from the artist to all of us.

I want to thank Diane Stanley for these wonderful pictures. If people look at them thoughtfully and follow the thread of meaning through the series, they may be encouraged, inspired, and guided in their own process.

The Meanings of "Meaning"

I still remember well first reading Victor Frankl's inspiring book *Man's Search for Meaning* many years ago when I was a high school student. It left an indelible impression in my memory. Frankl's story of survival in the death camps and his subsequent creation of logotherapy constitute one of the 20th century's great stories of human endurance and resilience. His is a theory tested in the fires of extreme experience. As he discovered, a sense of meaning matters — for our very survival. My later interest in psychoanalysis, specifically in Jungian thought and practice, had its earliest inspiration in Viktor Frankl's *Man's Search for Meaning* and in Freud's *Interpretation of Dreams*, which I read also in my adolescence. It was with great pleasure, therefore, that I accepted the invitation to speak at this conference on the topic of "Motivation and Meaning." I will do so from the perspective of Jungian psychology, its theory and practice, since this has been my professional location for the past 45 years. To be honest, Jung has been a core part of my personal sense of meaning and has powerfully motivated me to dedicate my professional activities to writing, teaching, and clinical practice in the field of analytical psychology.

To begin, let me pause for a moment and recognize that "meaning" is a word. Following the guidance of Wittgenstein on language, I will take a look at how this word is used within the context of analytical psychology. In Jungian circles, we use the word "meaning" quite a lot. The question is: How do we use it, and what do we intend to say when we use it? Often it is brought into play when we speak of dreams or numinous experiences, but it also comes up in the everyday sense when we speak about relationships, love, work, career, hobbies, and so forth.

Psychologically, we usually use the word, "meaning," to refer to a conscious feeling or a subjective judgment. We speak of "a sense of meaning." A certain activity or a general set of ideas and actions gives us "a sense of meaning." To say that "meaning" is a word that refers to a specific feeling is not to diminish its value or importance. Our feelings are what we live with most of the time, and they often govern our choices and decisions about how to live, whom to live with, and in general, they set the tone of our everyday lives. Psychotherapists spend a lot of time reflecting on feeling with their patients. Feelings make a difference. A "sense of meaning" is a positive feeling and something most people want in their lives.

Sometimes, however, we also speak of "meaning" as archetypal, that is, as transcendent to consciousness, inhering in the collective unconscious and ultimately delivered to the conscious subject by the objective Self. In this sense, meaning is spoken of not as a conscious feeling but an attribute of a psychological constellation whose source lies outside consciousness.

On the one hand, then, we speak about "meaning" as subjective, as when we say we have "a sense of meaning"; on the other hand, we speak of "meaning" as objective, i.e., as transcendent to conscious feeling or judgment, as when we say that a synchronistic event (a meaningful coincidence) has occurred. The one is an immediate feeling in consciousness, and the other is delayed and arrives in consciousness by way of reflection. The second carries a reference to transcendence. Its source transcends the ego and arrives as a gift of grace.

I will reflect on the relation between these two types of meaning. A question to be considered is this: Must a subjective "sense of meaning" participate in objective "transcendent meaning" in order to maintain its power of conviction and motivation? Will a subjective sense of meaning be able to sustain itself as motivational without support from a source beyond the limitations of the subject and transcendent to the ego?

I have to say, however, that even the mere suggestion of transcendent meaning is highly problematic for contemporary women and men. By "contemporary," I mean postmodern in sensibility and outlook. We live in an age that has totally banished myth and metaphysics from serious consideration. In postmodernity, we can freely play with myth and speculative imagination, but we do not bind our will and destiny to them as people did in other times and places. We look on such affirmations as premodern or pathological. We must ask, therefore: Can a person find a sustainable sense of meaning, which may require a transcendent anchor, while at the same time actively participating in a culture such as ours that rejects religious symbols and beliefs as points of orientation? On a collective level, we have no master narratives that connect us to the gods, to the infinite, to the eternal. In this cultural situation, what can sustain a sense of meaning for the individual? Will it not collapse — like a transient mood? For many people, this is the case.

I will speak now of how analytical psychology addresses this problem and I will use Jung's recorded experiences as a model. I do this because it is in the public record and so does not violate rules of confidentiality that ordinarily apply to clinical cases.

It is well known that Jung set out on a search for meaning by going on a quest for a myth to live by when, after writing his defining departure from Freud, *Wandlungen und Symbole der Libido*, he confronted himself and starkly realized that he no longer subscribed to the Christian creed or myth. He suddenly found himself in a vacuum of meaninglessness. What followed was the Red Book period, a deep dive into the life of the imagination. It was a passionate search for what he called "a personal myth" that could provide and sustain a sense of meaning for him.

What is a personal myth? In general, myth is a collectively accepted narrative structure of image and thought that implies transcendent reference to objective meaning that lies beyond the groping attempts of mere subjectivity. The eternal gods offer finite mortals a point of reference to transcendent meaning that is absolute and not subject to time and change. Myths are like the stars that guide the mariner across the high seas.

A personal myth is an individually experienced structure of image and narrative that also implies transcendence and objective meaning in the background of a subjective sense of meaning. Myth anchors the relative and time-bound subject's sense of meaning in the absolute. A personal myth like a collective myth provides a foundational level of certainty and security for a subjective sense of meaning, like the gold bars kept in the vaults of the Swiss federal bank to back up the country's paper currency. Still, the idea of personal myth sounds strange because we generally think of myth as belonging to a group and having a long history to which the individual is an heir.

Toward the beginning of his *Liber Novus* and at the outset of his journey through the archetypal world of imagination, Jung inscribes a key passage that speaks of the topic of meaning. He writes about a conversation with a figure named simply, Soul, a feminine presence who has confronted and questioned him and has made some demands.

> On the following night I had to write down all the dreams that I could recollect, true to their wording. The meaning of this act was dark to me. Why all this? Forgive the fuss that rises in me. Yet you want me to do this. What strange things are happening to me? I know too much not to see on what swaying bridges I go. Where are you leading me? Forgive my excessive apprehension, brimful of knowledge. My foot hesitates to follow you. Into what mist and darkness does your path lead? *Must I also learn to do without meaning*? If this is what you demand, then so be it. This hour belongs to you. *What is there, where there is no meaning*? *Only nonsense, or madness*, it seems to me. Is there also *a supreme meaning*? *Is that your meaning, my soul*?[1] ("Was ist, wo kein *Sinn* ist? Nur *Unsinn* oder *Wahnsinn*, so scheint mir.

---

[1] C.G. Jung, *The Red Book: Liber Novus*, pp. 137-8. Italics added.

201

> Gibt es auch einen *Übersinn*? Ist das
> dein *Sinn*, meine Seele?"[2])

This passage sets the stage for all that is to come in *Liber Novus*. Soul is demanding that he put aside his acquired conscious "sense of meaning" for a time, which would derive from his previous work as a psychiatrist and author and from his family life and friendships. He is being asked to venture into the unknown without the security offered by his professional positions and achievements. There, he might discover Soul's meaning, i.e., supreme meaning (*Übersinn*).

I want to call special attention to three key words in this passage: "meaning" (*Sinn*), "nonsense" (*Unsinn*) and "supreme meaning" (*Übersinn*). The first two belong to the conscious world of the narrator (the ego, or "I," in the story), who is a middle-aged Swiss psychiatrist and scientific researcher, and the third is suggested by the Soul (a symbolic figure of the collective unconscious, portrayed in the text as a woman and which Jung would name in his later psychological theory "anima"). The narrator in this story ("I") is willing to let go of his limited sense of meaning even though it throws him into a confused state of mind where nonsense and madness threaten to consume him. But he tentatively trusts that Soul will provide another, or a different, sense of meaning, namely "supreme meaning" (*Übersinn*). This will be an attribute of the personal myth he is seeking to discover in this journey to the interior of the psyche.

What kind of meaning (*Sinn*) is typically available to the subject? This would be the sort that we find in our everyday lives as we invest in our activities and relationships.

---

[2] C.G. Jung, *Das Rote Buch*, p. 148. Italics added.

We don't have to search far for it. It is at hand. It comes along with our activities and achievements. If we have a satisfying job, for instance, and do well in it, a sense of meaning will be a side effect. Or if we see our children grow and do well, we will say that participating in family life and contributing to the well-being of loved ones gives us a sense of meaning. This type of meaning is a feeling that is derived from our activities.

This sense of meaning has many levels and can imply the archetypal layer in the psyche. A person might say to her therapist: "I went to the exhibition of contemporary art in Basel. I found it very meaningful." She is saying that it caught her interest, that it spoke to her in some way that was of personal significance, perhaps that it reminded her of vaguely felt but profound associations and feelings. It is hard for her to define more clearly what she means by "meaningful," but clearly this has to do with a feeling of the significance of the experience for her. This could be a transitory feeling that will fade in a short while, or it might be something more significant, a deeper sense of meaning. It could even touch upon the archetypal level of her psyche. A psychology of deep meaning is a symbolic psychology, a psychology of soul and the depths of the collective unconscious. It speaks of symbols and their powerful, even numinous, effect on our emotions and consciousness. Such experiences of feeling can change our lives and send us in new directions. This level of meaning has irrationally derived motivational power. The meaning here gives us a will to live.

Sometimes, however, the sudden eruption of a sense of meaning in such numinous experience looks, in retrospect, like a psychotic episode. This is especially true when it is not linked to other more mundane aspects of the sense of meaning in life and work. I recall a patient who came to me one day for a therapy session and claimed that he had seen just that morning a number of highly meaningful symbols in the trees around his house. I asked him what he had seen and what this meant to him. He said that he had seen crosses carved into the bark of the trees and that these were signaling his identity as Jesus Christ. Normally, he was a polite and somewhat detached churchgoer who regularly attended a Protestant church on Sunday mornings: Nothing more mystical than that. At this point in his life, he was a retired businessman with a few minor hobbies that he enjoyed to pass the time. But on this day, he smiled at me in a knowing way, believing that I could now too recognize him as the Christ. We spoke about this quietly through the session, and I neither contradicted nor agreed with him. He did not seem in any danger. When I saw him again a week later, he had returned to his normal state of consciousness and did not refer to this episode again. It had faded away, and he now once again functioned as a more or less rational person living in the modern secular world. Nevertheless, it is quite possible, even likely, that his identification with the Christ symbol continued to lie dormant in his unconscious and would continue to offer a sense of transcendent meaning in his life, but in a more subdued way. Even if it was extreme, this experience was not pathological in the sense that it interfered with his normal life. He had momentarily been in the grips of a powerful collective mythic symbol to which supreme meaning (*Übersinn*) is attached.

There is a similar episode recorded in *Liber Novus,* when Jung identifies momentarily with the Crucified Christ figure. In retrospect some 12 years later, Jung interprets this episode in a seminar given to his students and says of it:

> In this deification mystery you make
> yourself into the vessel, and are a vessel
> of creation in which the opposites
> reconcile. The more these images are
> realized, the more you will be gripped
> by them. When the images come to you
> and are not understood, you are in the
> society of the gods or, if you will, the
> lunatic society; you are no longer in
> human society, for you cannot express
> yourself. Only when you can say, "This
> image is so and so," only then do you
> remain in human society. Anybody
> could be caught by these things and lost
> in them – some throw the experience
> away saying it is all nonsense, and
> thereby losing their best value, for these
> are the creative images. Another may
> identify himself with the images and
> become a crank or a fool.[3]

In short, from such experiences a sense of "supreme meaning"
can be forged if they are linked to the rest of a person's life
and incorporated into a subjective sense of meaning.

The more ordinary sense of meaning can apply to
anything — to cleaning out closets, to shopping for a dress,
to cooking, to mowing the lawn and working in the garden.
It is a feeling of pleasure, and it oils the wheels of the psyche
like petroleum in the gears of an automobile engine. This

---

[3] C.G. Jung, *Analytical Psychology*, p.99.

mundane sense of meaning signifies that psychic energy is flowing smoothly into everyday life. We say that libido is in progression. Sometimes this is small and seemingly mundane, and sometimes it is more symbolic and even numinous. Here, the soul is actively present (the anima is "the archetype of life itself," according to Jung). When the soul is awake and active in our lives, we feel motivated to get up in the morning and go about our business with a positive, even a joyful, attitude.

Consider the opposite situation. A client says to his therapist: "I just can't bear to go to my job anymore. It has no meaning. It is empty, routine, boring. It grinds me down to dust." His work is tedious and no longer attracts his libido. It has lost its shine, and he has fallen out of love with his tasks and the workplace environment. The sense of meaning is absent. This happens frequently. This is what we call "burnout." It is not really a clinical depression, but rather ennui, "acedia." It can get worse and become more general as "sloth," one of the seven deadly sins. This signals the absence of anima in daily life. Now the libido disappears and flows backward into the unconscious. This is the mode of regression, and it will almost inevitably produce important and meaningful dreams that eventually suggest a new direction in life and bring a new sense of meaning.

The direction of libido fluctuates, and this gives and takes away the sense of meaning in our daily activities. We are dependent on this flow for our sense of meaning. Often, we are helpless in the face of these fluctuations. They come and go as life happens to us.

The person who finds himself in the condition of burnout is the opposite of someone who feels "called," who has a strong and vibrant sense of vocation, who feels that his tasks, even if mundane and routine on the surface, relate to a sense of purpose. This may relate to raising children or working in the executive suite of a large corporation. A sense of vocation motivates a person to go to work every day with energy and a positive feeling about the day ahead. Such a person is in the "flow," as Mihaly Csikszentmihalyi says. Being in the "flow" indicates energy, motivation, pleasure, and meaning associated with a specific activity. Mathematicians will find it in doing their calculations, lovers in their affairs, physicians in their surgeries.

This is the type of meaning that is available to the subject when psychic energy is flowing progressively and oriented by symbols. It should be noted, however, that this type of meaning also is not created by the subject. The subject receives the sense of meaning as an effect of libido's flow into actions that draw it forward. Meaning is offered as an effect of libido's progressive flow; it is a gift. And it can vanish. Love can suddenly or gradually fade away; interest in one's work and the sense of vocation can evaporate in certain circumstances. In psychotherapy, we face these situations on a regular basis. Meaning is suddenly lost after an accident or loss, and every possible action seems to be nonsense. There is no longer any motivation to continue along a given path in life. And when it is lost, it becomes strikingly apparent that a sense of meaning is essential for motivation. The subject cannot go on very well without it. Everything seems mechanical. It is nonsense (*Unsinn*). This was Jung's condition when he lost his relationship with Freud, as he recounts in *Memories, Dreams, Reflections*: "After the parting of the ways with Freud, a period of inner uncertainty began for me. It would be no exaggeration to call it a state of disorientation. I felt totally suspended in mid-air..." It was at this moment that he asked himself:

> ... in what myth does man live nowadays? In the Christian myth, the answer might be, "Do you live in it?" I asked myself. To be honest, the answer was no. For me it is not what I live by. "Then do we no longer have any myth?" "No, evidently we no longer have any myth." "But then what is your myth, the myth in which you do live?" At this point the dialogue with myself became uncomfortable, and I stopped thinking. I had reached a dead end.[4]

This was the beginning of his search for meaning at midlife.

As we saw in the Red Book experience quoted above, Jung was asked by "Soul" to recall and write down his dreams. At first, he did not understand why he should do this. It seemed like nonsense, irrelevant, silly — in other words, meaningless. Nevertheless, he complied with Soul's instruction and did record two important dreams from his childhood. They are recorded in his autobiography, *Memories, Dreams, Reflections*:

> ... I was in a dark wood that stretched along the Rhine. I came to a little hill, a burial mound, and began to dig. After a while I turned up, to my astonishment, some bones of prehistoric animals. This interested me enormously, and at that

---

[4] C.G. Jung, *Memories, Dreams, Reflections*, p. 171.

moment I knew: I must get to know nature, the world in which we live, and the things around us.

There came a second dream. Again I was in a wood; it was threaded with watercourses, and in the darkest place I saw a circular pool, surrounded by dense undergrowth. Half immersed in the water lay the strangest and most wonderful creature: a round animal, shimmering in opalescent hues, and consisting of innumerable little cells, or of organs shaped like tentacles. It was a giant radiolarian, measuring about three feet across. It seemed to me indescribably wonderful that this magnificent creature would be lying there undisturbed, in the hidden place, in the clear, deep water. It aroused in me an intense desire for knowledge, so that I awoke with a beating heart. These two dreams decided me overwhelmingly in favor of science, and removed all my doubts.[5]

These dreams, as he says, instilled his motivation to pursue science over philosophy in his studies and later in his career. Writing them down again, now at the age of 38, reminded him of his vocation as a scientist.

---

[5] *Ibid.*, p. 85.

Without doubt, the sense of vocation is one of the most important sources of a sense of meaning in a person's life. It is a great motivator. Vocation is a calling, and the Caller is the Self. The subject receives a calling from a source beyond itself, an inner source that is irrational. In religious language, the Caller is God. This anchors the subject's personal sense of meaning in supreme meaning. People do things out of an emergent sense of vocation that often they cannot explain or justify. They say they simply must do them. Recalling these dreams of his youth brought Jung back to the sense of vocation that had guided him to a meaningful life up to this point. But now he needed something more, something specific and attuned to his present situation. It now became a matter of finding a new path where the old one had given out but along the same vocational lines. Jung would always be a physician and a scientist, but he had to readjust his vision. He needed to find a myth that could anchor his future work in supreme meaning. His personal sense of meaning from here forward would depend upon it.

In speaking of searching for "a myth to live by," we are taking a step further on the quest for a sense of meaning. We are looking for a higher order structure, for what *The Red Book* refers to as "supreme meaning" (*Übersinn*). What is this "supreme meaning"? It would seem to be something transcendent.

There often comes a moment in life, usually around midlife as it did in Jung's case, when many things that once had a sense of meaning now seem like nonsense, outgrown, and lacking in the meaning they once had. This is not exactly the same as burnout, which can often be resolved with some rest and time out. It can instead be an ongoing crisis that needs considerable time and inner work to become resolved. One is not approaching the problem as soluble on the same level. It implies a new starting point on the level of archetype, not of ego. This takes time to emerge from the collective unconscious. In the meantime, there is liminality, a period of waiting and watching what appears in dreams and other irrationally motivated and directed experiences. In this situation, Jung chose to listen to "the spirit of the depths" and not "the spirit of this time." In other words, he looked inward and began his journey through the unconscious by way of active imagination.

This same thing happens to entire collectives or cultures as well as to individuals. Symbol systems, i.e., myths, that at one time in history carried vast collective and transcendent meaning for people, lose their numinosity and become nothing more than dead artifacts, cultural curiosities, antiquities, even embarrassments. This is what has happened in the West over the last couple of centuries to the traditional religions. The deep reservoir of meaning offered by Christianity and its symbols has dried up. The priceless paintings hung on the walls of the great cathedrals are admired for their artistic value, aesthetically, but they no longer induce mystical states of contact with the Divine. The great cathedrals of the Middle Ages have become museums. The sense of supreme meaning once resident in them has vanished, and while the paint remains on the altars and the canvases, the soul has fled elsewhere. This has thrown Western postmodern culture into a state of liminality: "liquid modernity," as the philosopher Zygmunt Bauman has called it. We are afloat in this milieu as we search for new guiding myths and collective narratives that will offer a sense of supreme meaning.

This phenomenon of transcendent meaning "fading away" from collective consciousness has happened to religions of the world in many times and places. When the numinosity of ancient pagan religions faded into curious metaphors that held little conviction, Christianity filled the void and offered a new set of symbols that offered a sense of transcendent meaning. Today in Europe and North America, many of the churches and cathedrals of Christendom are museums, collections of aesthetic objects like stained glass windows and beautifully carved altars. They draw tourists but not worshippers. The soul has left and gone elsewhere in search of meaning. What does a culture do when transcendent meaning has left, when it is hollowed out and nothing is left but concerns about material comfort and entertainment?

For individuals and collectives, this spells a time of crisis. We are in such a time in our cultural history. Modernity prepared the way, and postmodernity has advanced it. Sports events have much more meaning for many people than religious rituals. In a sense, they are religious rituals in secular dress and have some temporary meaning-giving effect, but a sense of transcendent meaning is absent. This means it must be repeated over and over again to maintain its meaning-giving power. Today's football victory becomes a stale memory tomorrow. In the 19th century the numinous left religion for many people and passed over into art. "God is dead" was pronounced, but Richard Wagner's operas carried the aura of the numinous, and the theater at Bayreuth became a place of worship. Today, the great art museums in New York, London, and Paris act as cathedrals, and so do shopping malls. What they do not claim explicitly, however, and cannot in our postmodern times, is transcendent meaning. In postmodernity, transcendence is a mere idea, and mostly a severely suppressed one.

Übersinn, however, *is* transcendent meaning. It is objective, not subjective. It is beyond "a sense of meaning." This is meaning that exists beyond the realm of conscious understanding. It may be delivered by symbols. Symbols express meaning that cannot be articulated by the intellect. They are windows to the soul. Do we have such experiences today? Peter Berger wrote of "signals of transcendence," moments of symbolic meaning that happen spontaneously, unannounced and unexpected, anywhere and at any time. This was also Rudolf Otto's experience. In the numinous experience, he sensed an invisible power, a *mysterium tremendum et fascinans*.

I recall the dream of a young man who came to me for some sessions of analysis. He had been an orphan and was adopted at the age of 4 by a childless couple. Now at the age of 30, he was struggling with the question of meaning and vocation. He was uncertain about his direction. Then, he brought a dream to a session in which he was visiting Istanbul and was in the magnificent Hagia Sophia, a place he had actually experienced on a trip not long before the dream. As he was walking in the cathedral under the dome, he looked up and saw the heavenly scene of the Father God surrounded by other figures. Then, he saw the Father coming lower in the dome and he felt himself ascending. As they approached one another, the Father looked him in the eye, pointed his finger toward him, and said in a grave voice that echoed throughout the space: "I want you!" The young man woke with tears in his eyes. As he told me the dream, we both had tears in our eyes. He felt "chosen," as he had been chosen at the age of 4 by his adoptive parents. Only now, the figure choosing him was transcendent, and this would become a ground for his personal myth as he went forward into the rest of his life. A pattern was repeating itself in his life: being chosen.

Jung found a way of theorizing about transcendent meaning in his writings on synchronicity. Jung defined synchronicity as a "meaningful coincidence," a convergence of an inner event like a dream or intuition and an outer event. He gives a number of examples of this from his clinical practice. Inevitably, these coincidences struck the chord of a type of meaning that is not man-made or constructed. What type of meaning is this? Not all coincidences are meaningful, but when they are, then the element of meaning is delivered by the convergence of causally unrelated events and is perceived by the subject as having meaning. Jung speaks of synchronicity as a special case of "acausal orderedness"[6] which includes "factors such as the properties of natural numbers and the discontinuities of modern physics." He continues: "... we must regard them as creative acts, as the continuous creation of a pattern that exists from all eternity, repeats itself sporadically, and is not derivable from any known antecedents."[7] The meaning contained in synchronistic events is in the pattern that is anchored in a transcendent process of creativity, which is repeated in time unpredictably. From Jung's account in his writings, including his autobiography, we can see that he considered synchronicity to be an essential element in

---

[6] C.G. Jung, "Synchronicity: An Acausal Connecting Principle," *CW* 8, para. 965.
[7] *Ibid.*, para. 967.

the creation of a personal myth, a myth to live by. Behind synchronicity lay the self as "the archetype of orientation and meaning. ... For me, this insight signified an approach to the center and therefore to the goal. Out of it emerged a first inkling of my personal myth."[8] This realization of a personal myth was backed by a number of synchronicities that anchored it securely in "supreme meaning."

In Jungian work, the process of forming a personal myth is made up of a combination of passive waiting (*Wu wei*, as the Taoist masters call it) and active engagement with dreams, images, and synchronistic events. The subject arrives at the sense of meaning, personal and transcendent, by paying careful attention to these data. It is a process with many ups and downs, twists and turns. "The way is serpentine," as Jung describes the individuation journey. It includes sense and nonsense and supreme meaning, and at any given moment, we can be in touch with any one of these meanings of meaning.

Conclusion

I would like to close this talk with a passage from *Memories, Dreams, Reflections* that speaks in moving terms of the meaning of human consciousness itself within the cosmos. In this reflection, Jung gives humankind a standing that is coequal with the Creator. The human contribution has to do with the realization of meaning in nature. This would also speak to our ecologically sensitive time.

In the chapter titled "Travels," Jung tells of his experiences in many parts of the world outside Europe, and

---

[8] C.G. Jung, *Memories, Dreams, Reflections*, p. 199.

among them is his account of his journey in 1925 to Kenya and Uganda (pp. 253-274). Toward the beginning of that trip, he had the opportunity to step out of the company he was with and take some time apart and alone. He writes:

> ... I walked away from my companions until I had put them out of sight, and savored the feeling of being entirely alone. There I was now, the first human being to recognize that this was the world, but who did not know that in this moment he had first really created it. ... There the cosmic meaning of consciousness became overwhelmingly clear to me. "What nature leaves imperfect, the art perfects," say the alchemists. Man, I, in an invisible act of creation put the stamp of perfection on the world by giving it objective existence. ... Now I knew... that man is indispensable for the completion of creation that, in fact, he himself is the second creator of the world, which alone has given to the world its objective existence — without which, unheard, unseen, silently eating, giving birth, dying, heads nodding through hundreds of millions of years, it would have gone on in the profoundest night of non-being down to its unknown end. Human consciousness created objective existence and meaning, and man found

his indispensable place in the great
process of being.[9]

In this quiet moment and alone in the vast savannah, Jung discovered the meaning of human consciousness and tied it into his sense of supreme meaning within the cosmic structure of Creation itself. This, too, became an important piece in his myth of meaning. One could argue that it might provide a basis for a collective myth of meaning for all of humanity in our time. Humans are not existent because of meaningless chance and, as such, even a blight and a cancer on the face of our planet. We are here to bring the world to consciousness. This is our meaning in the great scheme of things. It is up to us to do something of significance with this sense of supreme meaning.

---

[9] *Ibid.*, pp. 255-56.

The Faith of the Analyst[1]

Faith is a mystery. Some people have it and some don't. It may depend on childhood and the presence of the good-enough mother who lays down a psychological foundation of trust. But paradoxically, I have also noticed that people who had health or serious emotional problems or traumas in their early years, sometimes even hovering between life and death and uncertain whether or not to stay in this world, often have an uncanny connection to mystical spirituality, another source of trust. It's as though the supernatural hovers about them and participation in another invisible world is an ever-present possibility. Sometimes, this frightens them, but if it does not, it can turn into faith in their destiny as individuals. If they become Jungian psychoanalysts, they often show a gift for sustaining the pressures of taking a deep dive into the unconscious with their patients. Their faith, which is based on personal experience of the transcendent, sustains them through thick and thin.

In this reflection, I will address several questions, all of which fall under the larger issue of the analyst's "faith" when working with the inevitable crises and moments of despair that arise in the course of analysis. The questions to be considered here are:

1) What is "faith"?
2) "Have I faith or a faith or not?" (the question Jung asked himself in a letter to Father Victor White, O.P.[2])

---

[1] Previously published in *The Journal of Analytical Psychology* 56:3, 2011. Here augmented and revised.
[2] A. Lammers, *The Jung-White Letters*, p. 119.

3) Does the presence or absence of faith on the part of the analyst make a significant difference for the course and outcome of analytic work?

Following the response to these questions, I will consider some typical moments of crisis that arise in analysis and are sketched briefly in Jung's essay "The Psychology of the Transference," where he writes: "The collapse and disorientation of consciousness may last a considerable time, and it is one of the most difficult transitions the analyst has to deal with, demanding the greatest patience, courage, and faith on the part of both doctor and patient."[3]

Question 1: What is "faith"?

I will begin by asking a basic question: What do we intend when we use the word "faith"? Within traditional religious contexts, "faith" has a clear metaphysical and supernatural reference. It means "faith in God" (or "Goddess") as named and revealed in the Sacred texts and rituals of the specific religion in which it is used. The English word's etymology, however, is actually devoid of explicit reference to anything religious or supernatural. In the Shorter Oxford English Dictionary, we find that the English word "faith" derives from the Latin *fides*, *fide-*, *fidere* and that the Latin *fides* translates the Greek *pistis*. The basic meanings of these Latin and Greek root words are: confidence, reliance, trust. This can be trust in anyone or anything — in one's own creative abilities and powers, for instance, as Louise Bourgeois, the famous sculptress, used the word when she was asked, "How were you able to continue working for so long without public recognition" (she

---

[3] C.G. Jung, "The Psychology of the Transference," para. 476.

was not "discovered" until she was in her 70s and had been busy as a sculptress for decades), and she said, "I just had faith in my work!"[4] One can have faith in one's business or intimate partner (to be reliable and "faithful"), or in one's political party or leadership. Here, faith is purely of this world and without any spiritual or religious connotation. It means confidence and trust in someone or something visible, knowable, tangible. It is more or less equivalent to "I trust you" or "Your handshake is as good as a legal contract." Faith is trust, pure and simple, in anyone or anything.

For most people, however, "faith" is taken in the religious sense of the word. Having "faith" speaks of reliance and trust in God, hence affirming contact with and knowledge about a supernatural Being. In the Hebrew Bible, the great exemplars of faith — such as Abraham who trusted God and left his home country to embark on a journey into the unknown, and Moses who trusted God to provide nourishment during the years of wandering in the wilderness — place their trust in Deity, not in their own powers or in anything mundane. Faith, in this sense of the word, exceeds the reach of reason and the requirement for evidence. It leaps to another type of cognition (as in Kierkegaard's famous "leap of faith") where existential risk is involved. It rests on intuitive knowledge or what we might call Gnosis.

In the New Testament, we find a classic definition of faith in this religious sense: "Now faith is the assurance of things hoped for, the conviction of things not seen. For by it the men of old received divine approval. By faith we understand that the world was created by the word of God, so that what is seen

[4] "Louise Bourgeois: The Spider, the Mistress and the Tangerine," a film by Marion Cajori and Amei Wallach, Zeitgeist Video, 2008.

was made out of things which do not appear."[5] Faith here means a kind of knowledge — of the unseen, of a supernatural and ultimate Power operating behind the scenes and responsible for there being something rather than nothing and for destiny both individual and collective. Additionally, in the New Testament faith in Christ is made the condition of the soul's salvation, an idea that was powerfully propounded by Martin Luther in the Protestant Reformation. Faith becomes the requirement for salvation and ensures one's blessed condition, if not always to one's physical satisfaction in this life, then surely to one's spiritual satisfaction in the next. Faith is not trust in just anything; it is trust specifically in Christ. And the mystery of faith is resolved by John Calvin in his notion of predestination: The people who have faith are blessed and given their capacity for faith by divine Providence. Faith itself is rooted in the transcendent.

This religious understanding of faith is what has been passed down through generations of people embedded in the biblical traditions, and so it is not surprising to find that it is this understanding of the term, rather than the more neutral one as indicated by the word's etymology, that has been adopted also by the more or less secular culture of the West. It is commonly understood that the content of "faith" is made up of: a) the conviction that invisible and supernatural forces are at work in nature; b) knowledge, based on "revelation," about how these forces affect and impact visible reality in time and space; and c) trust in them regarding the ultimate triumph of good over evil and salvation for the souls of the believers. The term "faith" belongs most authentically to the vocabulary of the religious, and its existence separates the faithful from the unbelievers.

---

[5] Hebrews 11:1-3.

No wonder, then, that modern people generally have shunned the term. Logical positivism, for instance, considered all faith statements to be nothing but superstition, basically discardable nonsense. Faith belongs to the Middle Ages, to the Age of Faith, which has now been superseded by the Age of Reason. In the period of high modernity (19th and 20th centuries), to have faith was generally considered premodern, meaning that the "believer" remained mired in the mythological stage of human consciousness and had not yet evolved culturally into the modern stage, which adamantly rejected the notion of the supernatural and committed itself to the methods of empirical science and logical rationality. Faith is not a word used in scientific discourse. In fact, it is anathema, to use another religious term. Banished!

As a modern man committed to scientific method and research, Jung struggled with the term "faith." In a letter to Father Victor White dated May 21, 1948, he questions himself and writes: "Your paper ["Notes on Gnosticism"] has made me think: *Have I faith or a faith or not?* I have always been unable to produce faith and I have tried so hard, that I finally do not know any more, what faith is or means. I owe it to your paper, that I have now apparently an answer: faith or the equivalent of faith with me is what I would call *Respect.* I have respect of the Christian Truth. ... There is however nothing specific in it, since I feel the same kind of respect for the basic teachings of Buddhism and the fundamental taoistic ideas."[6]

Typical of cultural moderns and trained scientists, Jung has great difficulty with the term "faith." To his mind, it generally meant "belief" — assent to a particular set of doctrines and creeds be it Protestant Reformed, Roman Catholic, Moslem, Jewish, Hindu,

---

[6] A. Lammers (ed.), *The Jung-White Letters*, p. 119.

or whatever. It does not necessarily imply a firsthand, primary religious experience or a hard-won and rigorous philosophical position that includes a personal cosmological vision or, as Jung would say, a personal *Weltanschauung*. Jung could not identify with any of the traditional Confessions, even though he was culturally a Swiss Reformed Protestant. This kind of faith — sheer belief — Jung could not claim for himself, and indeed he often expresses hostility and defiance if pressed to accept authoritative teachings about transcendent or metaphysical teachings about God. But he did *respect* the religious traditions, all of them, and he learned a good deal from many. For him, they were loaded with archetypal symbolism and taught him about the contents of the collective unconscious. He did not subscribe to their ontological and metaphysical claims, however, and so he did not have "faith" in any of them. One could say that he looked at all of them from the outside with an unprejudiced gaze, and from this perspective, all were of equal value — for psychology. If he could replace "faith" with "respect," he was content. He did have genuine appreciation for religious thought and experience of all kinds.

But how "modern" was Jung, really, if we define "modern" as the absolute rejection of anything numinous, spiritual, or transcendent? He is very hard to pin down and capture in the familiar terms we use nowadays to categorize historical types of attitude and thinking — "premodern," "modern," and "postmodern." In contrast to what he says in this letter to Victor White just quoted, Jung *was* quite capable of expressing intuitions of transcendence — a kind of faith statement, I would argue — as they came to him spontaneously or through the channels of personal, and especially of numinous, experience. For instance, in a letter to Father White just prior to the one quoted above, he writes: "Whoever has clearly understood, what it means: *"Qui fidelis est in minimo"* ["He that is faithful in that which is least" (Luke 16:10)], is overwhelmed with the dura necessitas [hard necessity] of submission and discipline of a subtler kind than the regula S. Benedicti [Rule of St. Benedict]. I don't want to prescribe a way to other people, because I know that my way has been prescribed to me by a hand far above my reach."[7] Jung's caution here about giving advice to others is based on the sense that his own life has received direction and shape, indeed commands of a sort, from "a hand far above my reach." From this statement, it seems quite evident that he had given himself over in full submission to a "higher power," which, in other letters to White, he would freely refer to as God. Recall, too, the Delphic oracle inscribed over the doorway of Jung's own home: *Vocatus atque non vocatus Deus aderit* ("Called or not called, God is present") Here stood a constant reminder, as he entered his home day in and day out, of "Deus." Although it is hard to define and pin down precisely what this means, *Deus* is certainly a reference to a transcendent factor of which Jung was constantly reminded.

It is of this type of awareness of a "way," which "has been prescribed ... by a hand far above my reach," that I wish to speak in considering here the issue of faith and the practicing analyst. It is not faith in the conventional meaning of "belief" in traditional doctrines about God, but it is more than the neutral meaning of faith as simply trust in anyone or anything. It is faith rather in the sense of: 1) owning up to having an implicit or explicit recognition of Being that is more complete and comprehensive than our focused knowing can in principle ever comprehend or exhaustively understand; 2) trusting in the occasional glimpses we do have of this "hand far above my reach"; and 3) submitting to its greater vision, wisdom, will, and power. No more than Jung are

---

[7] *Ibid.*, p. 117.

most of us ready to accept without question authoritative teaching delivered from pulpit, mosque, synagogue, or cathedral. We value our freedom to think and to experience life for ourselves too highly for that. But do we go as far as he did in owning up to, trusting, and submitting to a "hand far above [our] reach"? I mean this as a challenge.

Leaving a specific, revealed God out of the picture, let's say that "faith" is defined as a kind of intuitive cognition, with strong emotional undertones and overtones, of a realm of being beyond our conscious grasp (awareness of "a hand far above my reach") and that it is forward-looking with trust ("the assurance of things hoped for"). Karl Jaspers used the neutral phrase "the Comprehensive" to speak of this realm toward which we would direct our attention in an act of faith.[8] The person of, or with, faith would put trust in such intuitive cognitions and, I would add, would do so because of personal experiences that suggest this totality is a Truth, a totality that exceeds the self of the individual person and is a kind of self of selves, an all-encompassing Self.

Question #2: "Have *I* faith or a faith or not?"

To this second question, each of us must give an individual and personal answer, quietly, inwardly, drawing on a personal anamnesis (to follow Eric Voegelin's example in establishing his noetic certainty and varieties of transcendences of consciousness[9]). We have to consult our memories, look back at the unfolding patterns in our lives, reflect on the question of meaning in the seemingly accidental twists and turns of our personal history (the "synchronicities"), and recall the "miracles."

---

[8] K. Jaspers, *Way to Wisdom*, pp. 28-38.
[9] E. Voegelin, *Anamnesis*, Chapter 3.

Speaking personally, therefore, I have to say that I have asked myself this question often and have answered it in different ways at various times in my life. As a child, I was exposed to religious faith in our home. I grew up with the Bible and became familiar with many of its stories and figures. Later, I studied Christian theology formally and intensively. And so, throughout my life, I have had many "phases" of being with and without, in and out of "faith" in the religious sense, depending on the phase of the individuation process I was in.

As I enter the later decades of life and ask myself this question, I find myself now drawing on a wealth of specific and what I call primary experiences, including important dreams, scenes and events from active imagination, and several astonishing synchronicities (I think of them as "miracles") that have shaped what I would now call my "faith platform." Of course, my reading in a wide variety of literatures has been important as well, but the primary experiences are the crucial elements. Considering these experiences, I can find also what Jung called "respect" for the religious traditions and for what people in them experience when they speak of "faith," but my own platform of faith is somewhat apart from the planks laid down by my own background religious tradition, Protestant Christianity.

Put into a few words and rather abstractly, my faith platform is that *time and eternity intersect and assure the transcendent value of certain numinous experiences, which in turn offer a deep sense of meaning for life.* I do recognize this as a variation on the notion of incarnation as affirmed in Christian faith, where an infinite God and a limited human consciousness unite in a specific historical moment. The element of numinosity in this moment is key. In my experiences, however, the Deity who is present in this moment is not always specified as the biblical one, although for me the symbol of Christ remains central.

Sometimes these numinous experiences of transcendent value have taken place in the *vas bene clausum* of analysis with my analysands. These are indelible "transformational moments"[10] for consciousness, and they have been recognized as such by both of us in the process. The intuition of an intersection or interpenetration of time and eternity, the finite and the infinite, the concrete and the symbolic, is the essence of this experience. It has a feeling of timelessness, and it communicates a sense of meaning that can be trusted for the present and the future. The hand behind the timing and exact location of these intersections is hidden in the Great Mystery. It is the "hand far above my head," as Jung says.

A satellite or derivative of this platform is the article (also of faith) that the individual human soul/psyche/self is of infinite value. Why? Because each finite person is a suitable subject for reception of the infinite. To my mind, this is what Jung meant by "the Christification of many" in his late work *Answer to Job*. Everyone is called to incarnate the infinite in this life; everyone is capable of receiving intuitions of the Divine and of finding ultimate meaning in life as lived concretely in each and every human context on the planet. Such Gnosis is freely available to every single person on Earth. The human self is an *imago dei* and therefore related to the Deity itself and graced with ultimate value. Whether the person realizes this or not, lives a short or a long life, individuates consciously or not, the value remains. So we "meet the Buddha" or "the Christ" in ourselves and in all the others we may encounter in our brief lives on earth. Rabbi Leo Baeck affirms

---

[10] I thank Linda Carter for this phrase in her article, "Countertransference and Intersubjectivity."

the same basic value from a Jewish perspective in his powerful essay "*Individuum Ineffible*," delivered at the Eranos Tagung in Jung's presence in 1947.

This also means that the human encounter with others, as we experience it in analysis, for instance, is of infinite potential. The horizontal interpersonal relationship, with all of its transference and projections, illusions and disillusionments, love and hate, and other dramas, is intersected by a vertical line of infinite value and potential for meaning that extends beyond the two empirical humans in this joint venture. In this we can trust.

Question #3: Does the presence or absence of faith on the part of the analyst make a difference for the course and outcome of analytic work?

Obviously, this makes a difference! Everything makes a difference if the analytic process becomes at all deep and transformative. The analyst's attitudes, temperament, cultural biases, complexes, personal development — all of these factors make a difference for the course and outcome of analysis because in the end they all enter into the process, affect the "field" and make an impact. But maybe it's useful to look a little more closely at how precisely this factor — faith, as I have defined it above — might make a crucial difference.

An analysand asked me recently at the beginning of a session and more or less out of the blue: "Do you believe we can change our fate, our destiny?" It was not clear to me where this question was coming from or why it was an issue. It is, of course, an impossible question on a scientific or rational level. What are destiny, fate? Do they really exist? To hold that each life has a destiny or a fate is itself a statement of faith and must be answered on the same level. And why would one want to change it? In reflecting on this question, I have to confess that I don't think we can interfere with an individual's destiny if that is what Jung meant by "a hand far above my reach." But we can come to accept it, even to love it (*amor fati*). For the analyst to take this position, however, requires an act of faith, namely that each individual's destiny is of value, even of ultimate value and meaning. Without this attitude engendered by faith, the analyst might be tempted to play God and try to help a person change his or her destiny. But where would that leave them? One thinks of the famous so-called Serenity Prayer by Reinhold Niehbuhr: "Father, give us courage to change what must be altered, serenity to accept what cannot be helped, and the insight to know the one from the other."[11]

"Only when God is there may one cease to be obliged to be God," wrote the German psychoanalyst and theologian Eugen Drevermann. It's a brilliant insight. For analysis to work properly, it seems to me, the analyst must not be cast in the role of God, but for this to be the case it is necessary to have a sense that the Transcendent is present in the room apart from either of the human participants, yet with them, among them, for here "two are gathered." Analysis takes place in the presence of the Divine and so participates in the sacred aura. In such a setting, even a very difficult fate can be accepted, appreciated, and found to be of ultimate value.

In this perspective, I often think of Jung's statement: "… the fact is that the approach to the numinous is the real therapy and inasmuch as you attain to the numinous experiences you are released from the curse of pathology. Even the very disease takes on a numinous character."[12] When even a disease — depression,

---

[11] https://yalealumnimagazine.com/articles/2709-you-can-quote-them
[12] G. Adler (ed.) *C.G. Jung Letters* 1, p. 377.

anxiety, addiction, borderline disorders, perversion — takes on a numinous character, it must mean that it has been placed within the infinitely containing perspective of faith.

What I would caution against is settling for something that sometimes, perhaps even often, happens when in classical Jungian terms, faith in the spiritual and religious sense of its meaning is translated simply as knowledge of the (invisible) archetypal world and the contents of the collective unconscious and trust in the self's processes. Jungian analysts routinely do employ this type of thinking when they treat patients, especially the challenging and difficult ones. They have faith in the psyche's wisdom, in the self's operations, even when these are opaque and hidden from view. From their training, they have some positive knowledge about the invisible world of the unconscious — they know of complexes and archetypal images and patterns of thought and behavior. They know about the self and about the ego's relativity with respect to the objective psyche. Without this knowledge, it would be difficult to proceed in many cases. But this falls short of faith as it is understood in the stronger sense, which implies knowledge of and trust in transcendent factors that lie entirely beyond the psychological realm and extend into what Jung called the psychoid dimension, and even beyond that to altogether transhuman or nonhuman material and spiritual dimensions of reality. Faith in this sense speaks of territory beyond the discernible ends of the spectrum that Jung uses as a metaphor to describe the human psyche, with the infrared shading off into the soma and the material world and the ultraviolet passing into the spiritual. Faith of this far reach passes beyond the personal, the causal, the rational, and looks to realms that Jung calls "the beyond" (*Jenseits*) in *The Red Book* and later discusses as the basis of synchronicity. The horizon of rationality of whatever kind is breached and opens out into the transpersonal and the cosmic. An image of such a glimpse into the cosmic world is depicted in the famous picture of the alchemist poking his head out of the globe and gazing at the supercelestial firmament of the stars, a firmament beyond even the physical stars. It is from here that our fate and our destiny are drawn. Our psyche is an *imago Dei*.

For modern people (like most of us) this is the sticking point: Is such knowledge possible, is it credible? For traditional religionists, it is possible only because of divine revelation, hence Anselm's famous sentence: "*Neque enim quaero intelligere ut credam, sed credo ut intelligam. Nam et hoc credo, quia, nisi credidero, non intelligam.*" ("Nor do I seek to understand that I may believe, but I believe that I may understand. For this, too, I believe, that, unless I first believe, I shall not understand.") But after Kant's critiques, we have become appropriately cautious about such certainties.

Yet Jung, quite sensitive to the Kantian caution, could also say, quite boldly, at the conclusion of his Terry Lectures at Yale in 1937: "... if the spiritual adventure of our time is the exposure of human consciousness to the undefined and indefinable, there would seem to be good reasons for thinking that even the Boundless is pervaded by psychic laws, which no man invented, but of which he has 'gnosis' in the symbolism of Christian dogma."[13] Clearly, he was intent on exploring beyond the bounds of the purely psychological realm, and of course, this attitude entered into his practice as an analyst.

Faith provides a quite specific perspective on the therapeutic process, in that it trusts that if the psyche/soul opens to the "unconscious" (which is without limit and cannot be defined exhaustively by the conscious mind) the necessary developments and movements for individuation will emerge. There is implicit trust that what is happening, however peculiar or bizarre at times, has

---

[13] C.G. Jung, "Psychology and Religion," *CW* 11, para. 168.

potential for meaning. The effect of this attitude on the part of the analyst is that analysands gain a sense of faith in themselves (in the self within themselves). The faith of the analyst, I would suggest, is subtly communicated and taken up in time by the analysand. The analyst's "I have faith that your psyche has infinite potential" becomes translated into "I have faith that my psyche has contact with the infinite and with its potential for meaning in my life."

Of course, in this era of evidence-based (and not faith-based) medicine and psychotherapy, it is necessary to offer studies and research that demonstrate results, that show that our methods work, that people benefit and get better, become more trusting of themselves, of their own feelings and intuitions. We need to be able to show that faith is communicable, that it passes from "I trust in you" to "I trust in the self."

There is a moving scene in Dante's *The Divine Comedy* when Virgil, who has accompanied the poet through Hell and Purgatory, takes his leave of Dante. He says to him:

> "My son," he said, "you now have seen the
> torment
> of the temporal and the eternal fires;
> here, now, is the limit of my discernment."[14]

Dante is now on his own as makes his way onward to Heaven. His guide, Virgil, has faith in his ability now to trust his own impulses, which have been cleansed and made conscious in the journey through Purgatory. He can now rely on his own connection to the Self. This does happen, too, in analysis, *Deo concidente.*

---

[14] Dante, *The Divine Comedy*, *Purgatorio* XXVII 127-143.

When "faith" is called for in analysis

There are phases of analysis, sometimes longer, sometimes shorter, when the analyst's faith in the process is tested. Jung writes about this quite explicitly and graphically in his essay "The Psychology of the Transference." In reference to Pictures 6 and 7 of the *Rosarium Philosophorum*, titled "The Ascent of the Soul," which he discusses at length in his work, he writes:

> This picture corresponds psychologically to a dark state of disorientation. The decomposition of the elements indicates dissociation and the collapse of the existing ego-consciousness. It is closely analogous to the schizophrenic state, and it should be taken very seriously because this is the moment when latent psychoses may become acute, i.e., when the patient becomes aware of the collective unconscious and the psychic non-ego. This collapse and disorientation of consciousness may last a considerable time and it is one of the most difficult transitions the analyst has to deal with, demanding the greatest patience, courage, and faith on the part of the doctor and patient. It is a sign that the patient is being driven along willy-nilly without any sense of direction, that is, in the truest sense of the word, he is in an utterly soulless condition ...[15]

What the analyst needs in this moment of the analytic process is, as Jung says, "faith." But faith in what? This is faith in the archetypal individuation process that is going through a passage of transition in which death and rebirth are the guiding powers. Death

---

[15] C.G. Jung, "The Psychology of the Transference," *CW* 16, para. 476.

appears strikingly in the analytic setting, either as loss of energy or confidence, or as depression that things are not improving but rather are getting worse, or as phantoms and dreams of death actually appearing to the patient's consciousness in an astonishing way and with the force of conviction. Patients are convinced they are about to die! Or they feel the presence of Death in their lives. Here, the analyst must hold on to the faith in individuation as an archetypal process. The analyst must be knowledgeable about the death-and-rebirth archetype. But this must be Gnosis, i.e., knowledge based on the analyst's own experience, otherwise it is not effective or strong enough to hold the analyst's confidence and trust in the process.

There are three typical types of crises that we as analysts face in our work with patients: a crisis of identity (shadow confrontation with accompanying shame and guilt); a crisis of "loss of soul" (anima disappears and leaves behind a cold and empty void); and a crisis of "loss of meaning in life" (animus flies away, leaving a blank space in cognition). Each one calls for a process of death and rebirth. And each one can challenge the analyst's faith in the individuation process.

Often, all three crises fall together in one dramatic period of life: the death of a close loved one with accompanying feelings of shame and guilt; the loss of social and/or professional status; a significant failure in business (bankruptcy) or relationship (divorce); a catastrophic medical diagnosis that suddenly presents the prospect of a short time to live or requires extreme medical treatment with limited chances of survival. As psychotherapists, we live constantly in the shadow of failure and death. We, too, are challenged to maintain a constructive attitude and a sense of meaning in what we do as caretakers of the soul.

If we look at how Jung came to his faith in transformation and personal Gnosis as described in *Liber Novus*, we see many encounters with the Dead and even with Death itself. In *Liber Novus*, Chapter VI of *Liber Secundus* titled "Death," Jung describes his encounter with a "figure" standing "on the last dune ... wearing a black wrinkled coat: he stands motionless and looks into the distance ... he is gaunt and with a deeply serious look in his eyes."[16] Thereafter follows a vision of a multitude of the dead rolling down the hills into the sea, and Jung witnesses the horrors of the Great War to come. He himself descends into the cold valley of the shadow of death, where he loses all hope in a new life to come. And then there comes the grisly experience of rebirth: "*Inter faeces et urinas nascimur*" ("We are born between feces and urine" — St. Augustine): "For three nights I was assaulted by the horrors of birth. On the third night, jungle-like laughter pealed forth, for which nothing is too simple. Then life began to stir again."[17] Jung speaks of his Phoenixlike rebirth: "When I comprehended my darkness, a truly magnificent night came over me and my dream plunged me into the depths of the millennia, and from it my phoenix ascended."[18]

It was from experiences of the death-and-rebirth archetype such as this that Jung and many other analysts following his leadership have forged their Gnosis. This is the experiential/existential ground of the analyst's faith in the individuation process.

---

[16] C.G. Jung, *The Red Book*, p. 263.
[17] *Ibid.*, p. 268.
[18] *Ibid.*, p. 265.

References for
Mystery of Transformation

Adler, G. (ed.). (1973). *C.G. Jung Letters*, Vol. 1. Princeton, NJ: Princeton University Press.

Atmanspacher, H. and Fach, W. (2013). "A Structural-Phenomenological Typology of Mind-Matter Correlations." *Journal of Analytical Psychology*, 58/2.

Baeck, L. (1948). *"Individuum ineffabile."* *Eranos — Jahrbuch 1947*. Zurich: Rhein-Verlag. English translation by Gabriel E. Padawer and Bernard H. Mehlman, with Alisa Rethy. Hebrew Union College Annual, Volume 91 (2020), pp. 261-301.Introduced by David Ellenson and Paul Mendes-Flohr.

Berger, P.L. (1969). *A Rumor of Angels: Modern Society and the Rediscovery of the Supernatural*. New York: Doubleday.

Bergin, T.G. (1976). *Dante*. Westport, CT: Praeger.

Bloom, H. (1995). *The Western Canon*. New York: Little, Brown.

Campbell, J. (ed.) (1955). *The Mysteries. Papers from the Eranos Yearbooks*, Vol. 2. New York: Pantheon Books.

Cambray, J. (2009). *Synchronicity: Nature and Psyche in an Interconnected Universe*. College Station, TX: Texas A & M University Press.

_____. (2014). "German Romantic Influences on Jung and Pauli." In *The Pauli-Jung Conjecture* (eds. H. Atmanspacher and C.G, Fuchs). Exeter, UK: Imprint Academic.

Carter, L. (2010). "Countertransference and Intersubjectivity." In *Jungian Psychoanalysis* (ed. M. Stein). Chicago: Open Court.

Connolly, A. (2015). "Bridging the Reductive and the Synthetic: Some Reflections on the Clinical Implications of Synchronicity." *Journal of Analytical Psychology* 60/2.

Corbin, H. (1998). *Alone with the Alone*. Princeton, NJ: Princeton University Press.

Dante, A. (2003), *The Divine Comedy*. Translated by John Ciardi. New York: New American Library.

Fordham, M. (1985). *Explorations Into the Self*. London: Academic Press.

Freud, S. (1930/1961). *Civilization and Its Discontents*. New York: W.W. Norton & Co.

Goethe, W. (2001). *Faust, A Tragedy*. Translated by Walter Arndt, Edited by Cyrus Hamlin. New York: W.W. Norton & Co.

Gray, R.D. (2002). *Goethe the Alchemist: A Study of Alchemical Symbolism in Goethe's Literary and Scientific Works*. Mansfield Center, CT: Martino.

Heisig, J. (1979). *Imago Dei*. Cranbury, NJ: Associated University Press.

Hick, J. (2013). *The Fifth Dimension: An Exploration of the Spiritual Realm*. London: Oneworld Publications.

Jaffé, A. (2021). *Streiflichter zu Leben und Denken C.G. Jungs*. Einsiedeln, Switzerland: Daimon Verlag.

Jaspers, K. (1951/2003). *Way to Wisdom*. New Haven, CT: Yale University Press.

Jung, C. G. (1916/1961). *Septem Sermones ad Mortuos*. *Memories, Dreams, Reflections*. Appendix v. New York: Vintage Books.

_____. (1925/1989). *Analytical Psychology: Notes of the Seminar Given in 1925*. Edited by William McGuire. Princeton, NJ: Princeton University Press.

_____. (1938/1969). *Psychology and Religion. CW*. Vol 11. Princeton, NJ: Princeton University Press.

_____. (1939/1969). "Psychological Commentary on 'The Tibetan Book of the Great Liberation.'" *CW*. Vol. 11. Princeton, NJ: Princeton University Press.

_____. (1944/1968). *Psychology and Alchemy. CW*. Vol 12. Princeton, NJ: Princeton University Press.

_____. (1946/1966). "The Psychology of the Transference." *CW*. Vol. 16. Princeton, NJ: Princeton University Press.

_____. (1948/1967). "The Spirit Mercurius." *CW.* Vol. 13. Princeton, NJ: Princeton University Press.

_____. (1950/1969). "Foreword to the *I Ching*." *CW*. Vol 11. Princeton, NJ: Princeton University Press.

_____. (1951/1968). *Aion: Researches into the Phenomenology of the Self. Coll. Wks*. 9ii. Princeton, NJ: Princeton University Press.

_____. (1952/1969). "Synchronicity: An Acausal Connecting Principle." *CW*. Vol. 8. Princeton, NJ: Princeton University Press.

_____. (1954/1969). "On the Nature of the Psyche." *CW*. 8, Vol. 8. Princeton, NJ: Princeton University Press.

_____. (1955-6/1970). *Mysterium Coniunctionis. CW.* Vol. 14. Princeton, NJ: Princeton University Press.

_____. (1961). *Memories, Dreams, Reflections.* New York: Viking.

_____. (2009). *The Red Book: Liber Novus.* A Reader's Edition. New York: W.W. Norton & Co.

_____. (2020). *The Black Books 1913-1932, Notebooks of Transformation.* Volume 6. New York: W.W. Norton & Co.

Jung, C.G. and Pauli, W. (1952/1955). *The Interpretation of Nature and the Psyche.* New York: Pantheon Books.

Kerényi, K. (1944/1955). "The Mysteries of the Kabeiroi." J. Campbell (ed.), *The Mysteries.* New York: Pantheon.

_____. (1941/1950). *Das Ägäische Fest.* Wiesbaden: Limes Verlag.

Klitsner, Y.S. (2015). "Synchronicity, Intentionality, and Archetypal Meaning Therapy." *Jung Journal* 9/4.

Lammers, A. (ed.) (2007) *The Jung-White Letters.* New York and London: Routledge.

Luk, C. (ed. and transl.). (1970). *Ch'an and Zen Teaching.* Berkeley, CA: Shambhala.

Meier, C.A. (ed.). (2001). *Atom and Archetype. The Pauli/ Jung Letters,* 1932-1958. Princeton, NJ: Princeton University Press.

Muramoto, S. (trans.) (1998). "The Jung-Hisamatsu Conversation (1958)." *The Couch and the Tree,* edited by Anthony Molino. London: Open Gate Press.

Neumann, E. (1952/1956). *Amor and Psyche. The Psychic Development of the Feminine.* Princeton, NJ: Princeton University Press.

_____. (1952/1989). "The Psyche and the Transformation of the Reality Planes, A Metapsychological Essay." *The Place of Creation*. Princeton, NJ: Princeton University Press.

_____. (1958/1989). "The Experience of the Unitary Reality." *The Place of Creation*. Princeton, NJ: Princeton University Press.

Otto, R. (1917/1958) *The Idea of the Holy*. Oxford, UK: Oxford University Press.

Pauli, W. (1953/1989). "The Piano Lesson." *Harvest* 48/2, pp. 122-134.

Santagata, M. (2016). *Dante: The Story of His Life*. Cambridge, MA: Harvard University Press.

The Chemical Wedding of Christian Rosenkreutz. (1991). Translated by Joscelyn Godwin. Introduction and Commentary by Adam McLean. Boston: Phanes Press.

The Rosary of the Philosophers. (1980). Edited with a Commentary by Adam McLean. Edinburgh, Scotland: Magnum Opus Hermetic Sourceworks.

Van Erkelens, H. and F. W. Wiegel. (2002). "Commentary on *The Piano Lesson*." *Harvest* 48/2, pp. 135-141.

Voegelin, E. (2002). *Anamnesis. On the Theory of History and Politics*. Columbia, MO: University of Missouri Press.

Von Franz, M.-L. (1992). *Psyche and Matter*. Boston and London: Shambhala.

_____. (2002). "Interview with Herbert van Erkelens." *Harvest* 48/2, pp. 142-148.

Wilkerson, S.Y. (2019). *A Most Mysterious Union: The Role of Alchemy in Goethe's Faust*. Asheville, NC: Chiron Publications.